THE WAIT

Encouragement for Single Women

NICOLE C. DOYLEY

Published by
www.ruthscompany.org

Printed in the United States of America

ISBN: 978-9978-362-31-0

Contents

Part 1—Single and Fulfilled

Part 2—Dating with Wisdom

FOREWORD BY J. LEE GRADY

When I first met Nicole Doyley during a ministry trip to New Hampshire, her husband Marvin was not in the picture. Nicole was a talented single woman living near an Ivy League campus. She was smart and musically gifted. She was writing a book. She had natural leadership skills and was able to engage a crowd with her humor and biblical insights. She traveled internationally. I could tell this woman was going places!

But unfortunately for Nicole—and for so many other single Christian women like her—she struggled because the church doesn't know what to do with gifted single females. Even though she had a position at her church, the ceiling was low and her options were limited. Most people assumed that Nicole would eventually discover her ultimate destiny only when her husband finally materialized.

After all, isn't that what women do? They wait for the man of their dreams.

And so Nicole waited. And waited. And waited.

As Nicole tells the story, she dreaded the possibility that she would be a single woman at 40. As it turned out, Marvin came into her life just before she hit that fateful age. But because of the long wait, Nicole learned some valuable lessons that became a vital part of her life message. And I am thrilled that those lessons are now in print in this important book.

Because I am the father of four daughters, I have wrestled with the pressures women face in our culture. I have known Christian women who were told to bury their dreams, forsake higher education, or completely lose their identity in order to pursue marriage. Is that really how God feels about women?

I have noticed a trend in many churches today: Women who are successful in business or in some professional field feel unwelcome, as if they might be an unhealthy influence on women with more "pure" domestic inclinations. But I have to ask: Where in the Bible does it say every woman must marry? And why should we encourage single women to waste the most productive years of their lives by waiting for romance when their unique talents could be harnessed for a holy purpose?

Nowhere in the Bible are we told that God's ultimate purpose for a woman is to find a mate and then reproduce. On the contrary, the Scriptures tell us that our lives can be made complete by only one thing: a constant, abiding relationship with Jesus Christ. This is true for both men and women—all of us are called to know Him. This is our ultimate destiny.

Of course God ordained marriage. It was meant to be a

wonderful blessing that includes romance, sexual intimacy and the deepest expression of human love. But God never intended for a woman to derive her value from a man or to base her worth on producing offspring. Neither marriage nor childbirth validates a woman's personhood, her character or her spirituality. A woman's identity is to be found in Christ alone.

God makes a woman complete, whether she has a husband and twelve children or if she remains single all her life. Christ is her life; she is betrothed to Him.

This is the message we should offer single Christians today. Rather than enticing them to serve the false idols of fulfillment, we should challenge them to surrender every aspect of their futures to God. The heart-cry of every unmarried Christian should be, "Lord, I'm willing to serve You no matter what. Regardless of whether I marry this year or stay single the rest of my life, I'll find contentment in You." That is the attitude of surrender that God is looking for in every heart.

This is the attitude I see in Nicole Doyley—and it is what qualifies her so uniquely to convey the message of this book to single women. She speaks with sensitivity because she has been there; she writes with compassion because she has wrestled with the pain, the loneliness and the frustrations of life as a single Christian. She can speak to your heart because she has been there.

I believe God gave Nicole this message because He wants her to mentor many women in a new understanding of why God made them and how they can discover their giftedness. I pray you will let your guard down and let the Holy Spirit use Nicole's words to heal and empower you.

J. Lee Grady, author
Fearless Daughters of the Bible
10 Lies the Church Tells Women
25 Tough Questions About Women and the Church

Introduction

THE WAIT

On a balmy day in June of 1988, I faced the cold, hard truth that I was about to graduate from college with no boyfriend and no prospects. Several of my friends would receive both a diploma and a diamond on that joyous June day, and I looked forward only to the piece of paper. My singleness obscured any sense of accomplishment. In fact, about a month afterward, I sat sobbing on the edge of my bed, envisioning spinster-hood while despair grew by the moment in my heart. A friend, who had married at the ripe, young age of twenty-two, sat next to me, searching for something to say.

> **MY SINGLENESS OBSCURED ANY SENSE OF ACCOMPLISHMENT**

All of a sudden, a flash of brilliance struck, and she ran for her Bible. In a moment, she returned with it and found in the back a yellowed, torn, life-changing piece of paper. Here is what it said:

On His Plan for Your Mate

Everyone longs to give themselves completely to someone—to have a deep soul relationship with another, to be loved thoroughly and exclusively. But God, to the Christian, says, "No, not until you are satisfied and fulfilled and content with living loved by Me alone. I love you, my child, and until you discover that only in Me is your satisfaction to be found, you will not be capable of the perfect human relationship that I have planned for you. You will never be united with another until you are united with me—exclusive of anyone or anything else, exclusive of any other desires and longings. I want you to stop planning, stop wishing, and allow Me to give you the most thrilling plan existing—one that you can't imagine. I want you to have the best. Please allow me to bring it to you—just keep watching Me, expecting the greatest things—keep experiencing the satisfaction knowing that I am. Keep learning and listening to the things I tell you.... You must wait.

Don't be anxious. Don't worry. Don't look around at the things others have gotten or that I've given them. Don't look at the things you think you want. You just keep looking off and away up to Me, or you'll miss what I want to show you.

And, then, when you're ready, I'll surprise you with a love far more wonderful than any would ever dream. You see, until you are ready, and until the one I have for you is ready, I am working even this very minute to have both of you ready at the same time. Until you are both satisfied exclusively with Me and the life I have prepared for you, you won't be able to experience the love that exemplifies your relationship with Me...and this is perfect love.

And dear one, I want you to have this most wonderful love, I want you to see in the flesh a picture of your relationship with Me, and to enjoy materially the everlasting union of beauty and perfection and love that I offer you with Myself. Know I love you utterly. I am God Almighty. Believe and be satisfied.

I can quote most of that by heart. That summer day in my bedroom, those words came like cool lemonade to my soul. If I had known I would carry that paper around with me until I was forty years old, rehearsing it at least weekly while waiting for my mate, I would have jumped off a cliff (well, maybe not a cliff...). But God graciously never told me how long the wait would be. He rarely does. Our waiting times are almost always indefinite; how else would our faith grow? Our faith matures as we stand assured of what we hope for and convinced of what we do not see—for an indefinite amount of time. Look at Abraham and Sarah, who wound up waiting twenty-five years before God fulfilled the promise of a son.

I remember the time a visiting pastor laid hands on me and

started to pray. My heart pounded as I thought surely God would talk specifically about my man. He'd say something great like, "You're going to get married next year." Or maybe even next month. Though prophetic people often stay away from such predictions, maybe he would make an exception for me. But all he said was, "You've been waiting and waiting and waiting." Duh. "And there will be more waiting."

> OUR WAITING TIMES ARE ALMOST ALWAYS INDEFINITE; HOW ELSE WOULD OUR FAITH GROW?

Great. Thanks God. That's really encouraging. And then he spoke about exciting things I really didn't want to hear, like going to the nations as a spokesperson for the Kingdom. It was cool stuff, but I had tunnel hearing and only wanted to hear one thing. And it certainly wasn't wait!

God's ways surely are not our ways, but they are the best ways. (See Isaiah 55:8–9.) His design is so wonderful and so tailor-made for us that when we finally see the fulfillment of our prayers, all we can do is worship and thank Him.

I am so glad God made me wait. In those years, He did something so much more important than introduce me to my husband: He showed me that my life was about more than marriage. Ironically, it was the fact that I had a life, that I was active in so many different spheres and was developing my gifts and talents, that caused my husband to sit up and take notice when we first met. He didn't want someone who led a boring, purposeless life. He fell in love with a vibrant, active single woman who touched lives and pursued God. That is who I had become over eighteen years of waiting. Despite my kicking and screaming and crying and whining, God took His time to work in my heart—molding, breaking, and shaping me so that I would not only be ready for marriage but ready for His eternal purposes.

Back to that piece of paper. Over those years, the Lover of my soul made the words on that yellowing paper real in my heart.

What does it mean to be satisfied, fulfilled, and content? Can we really find satisfaction in God alone? I doubted it at first, but I eventually grew to see that this is God's desire for every person. Some learn it before they marry, and some learn it within their marriages, but all must learn it sometime in some way. I've also realized that even though God wants us to be content in Him, He also wants most of us married.

> **CAN WE REALLY FIND SATISFACTION IN GOD ALONE?**

So how do we achieve this happy state, even though all the while we're yearning for the companionship of a spouse? How do we hold all of that in balance? In the chapters that follow, we will discuss five ingredients for a fulfilled life, and then we'll talk about what to do with those persistent longings—while we wait.

Part 1
Single and Fulfilled

Chapter 1

INGREDIENT #1: BELIEVING YOU HAVE A DESTINY BIGGER THAN MARRIAGE

"I just really want to be a wife and mom," said the pre-med college student who had come over for tea during my son's nap. She wanted to chat about her career options and her new boyfriend, and she was much more excited about the boyfriend than a possible medical degree.

I had said the same thing during my early single years, and I've heard the same thing over and over from several young women. So many women, particularly Christian women, envision the house, the kids, the loving husband, the dog, and the yard. They think of the day when their days are filled with baking cookies, raising kids, and greeting their husband at the door after a long day's work—a *Leave it to Beaver* episode that plays and replays in their minds.

And, you know, there's nothing wrong with that. As a matter of fact, it's perfectly natural for women to daydream about weddings and husbands and kids. The problem is when that

> **YOU WERE MADE FOR MORE THAN A RING**

is all we dream about, when our dreams end at the altar and we think the wedding alone is our destiny.

You were made for more than a ring.

Now, I am not saying that every woman should work outside the home or that being a housewife is inferior to having a world-conquering career. I am saying, however, that even women who stay at home with their kids, see them off to college, and then become hands-on grandmothers still have a call on their lives that includes motherhood and other things. It could be taking in foster children, influencing the little girl next door who has no dad, giving to the poor, mentoring young moms, writing books, volunteering at the local shelter, or a multitude of other important things. The bottom line is, there is more to you than raising your kids and loving your husband, though of course these are extremely important.

As a single woman, it's your responsibility to find out what these other things are. Even if your greatest desire is to be married, open your mind and heart and start desiring something else, too. If you die tomorrow, will you leave anything significant behind, or are your days spent only in daydreaming and indulging in discontent?

EVEN IF YOUR GREATEST DESIRE IS TO BE MARRIED, OPEN YOUR MIND AND HEART AND START DESIRING SOMETHING ELSE, TOO

If you are in your thirties or forties or fifties and are not married, perhaps you are supposed to do something else before you wed. After you say, "I do," your time, energy, and money will be divided multiple ways. What can you throw yourself into now that will make a significant impact on an eternal soul?

The Highest Calling

I've heard it said that the highest calling is to be a wife and mother. I disagree. I think the highest calling for you is to be in the will of God. I certainly don't think that Gladys Aylward or Corrie Ten Boom were less important than my dear friend who stays home raising her seven children. These women are all heroines who have poured themselves out for other people and changed lives for the good.

> I THINK THE HIGHEST CALLING FOR YOU IS TO BE IN THE WILL OF GOD

When you are married, your husband and children will take priority over everything else, other than God Himself. But when you are single, what should occupy your thoughts? What is God calling you to? I know that He is whispering an assignment in your ear and trying to stir a passion in you other than the sexual passion you dream about. He has something for you to focus on other than the left ring finger of every man you meet. He has something for you to be excited about other than the "Hello" of the handsome bachelor in your office. He has something for you to be giddy and happy about other than a dinner invitation from the cute guy next door.

You're too smart to think only about your figure, and you're too precious to spend your days strutting your stuff and hoping for male attention. You are more than the number of nods you receive from men and the number of dates you've had this year. You are a princess, not a prisoner of singleness.

And do you want to know another sobering truth? Men don't like desperate women. Recently I was talking to an older single man and asked him why he wasn't married. He spoke about a few women he was dating, and I asked why he didn't pursue any of them seriously. "They're all too desperate; I don't like desperate women!" He went on to say that a few of them had asked him to marry them and even promised to provide for him financially. Oh brother! These are intelligent, attractive women, but their desperation for a man makes them totally unappealing for anything other than a good time. Desperation is like a man repellent. You can dress to kill and carefully dab on seductive perfume, but if you are desperate, you will ward off a lot of men.

> YOU ARE A PRINCESS, NOT A PRISONER OF SINGLENESS

Truly, a lot of singles are stunted.

Even though you're working and serving in the church, many of you have a hard time thinking about the bigger picture of your life.

I remember the day I was, for the four-hundredth time, bemoaning my singlehood. Another good friend (who also married enviously young) challenged me, "Nicole, what else do you want to be besides a wife? What does your life look like outside of the home?"

I sat dumb; I couldn't answer her! I always knew in my head that life was multifaceted, but I realized that deep down I was hoping a husband would be my panacea, my savior, not only from loneliness but also from purposelessness and boredom. My friend's question challenged me, and the Holy Spirit began to speak to me, "A husband will never give you purpose. Your life is about more than being a wife. Simply being a wife will never fulfill you."

That sobered me and propelled me to take hold of the garment of Jesus and beseech Him: "What have You called me to do? What have You made me to do? What can I do uniquely that no one else can do?"

Now, don't get me wrong; I haven't bought into the feminist ideals of the '70s and '80s that a woman should "bring home the bacon" by day, turn into supermom in the evening, and then transform one more time into a sexy, supportive wife at night. I never thought I could do it all, and I'm not encouraging you to try to do it all.

Nevertheless, that day I realized that even though I desperately wanted to get married, my life was meant to be about more than domestic bliss.

Singles in the Church

Sometimes the church world doesn't help. The family is so highly esteemed that, with no effort at all, one can conclude that life before marriage is suboptimal living; it's a winter season to be prayed through and left behind as quickly as possible.

WITH NO EFFORT AT ALL, ONE CAN CONCLUDE THAT LIFE BEFORE MARRIAGE IS SUBOPTIMAL LIVING

Winter literally is a season of death. The trees look dead; the grass looks dead; flowers are dead. Wildlife is hidden away and sleeping. Potential life lies dormant beneath the surface, but no life is visible. (I'm writing this in January, and all I see is dirty snow and naked trees.) How different the single life should be!

As a single woman, your life should be bursting with vitality and energy! You should be pursuing God, traveling, sowing eternal seeds in people's lives, and investing in your career and in those you love. The apostle Paul's life was so vibrant that he wished everyone was single so they could experience the fulfillment in God that he knew every day. Make that your aim. Decide that even if you long for a mate, nevertheless, those who look at you will see Spring, and you will indeed know life and fruit on a regular basis.

Sometimes Christians treat single women like they have some sort of disease. They keep them at arm's length and forget about them in their sermons, social gatherings, and prayers. Sermon illustrations are filled with examples appropriate for married people but totally irrelevant for singles. They can leave singles feeling lost and invisible. Churches organize all kinds of activities for stay-at-home moms and couples, but singles are left to fend for themselves. Or, worse, they are called on to provide childcare for the marriage activities. The problem is, because Christians believe in marriage (which is a good thing) many Christians get married very young, so they simply cannot relate to being thirty-five or forty-five or fifty-five and single. How many of you single women have had a married man ask,

> YOU SHOULD BE PURSUING GOD, TRAVELING, SOWING ETERNAL SEEDS IN PEOPLE'S LIVES, AND INVESTING IN YOUR CAREER AND IN THOSE YOU LOVE

"Why aren't you married yet?" As if you knew! As if you were supposed to pursue a man. As if you're somehow too prudish or too snooty or too picky or too something to get a man. You walk away sure that you must be the problem. You assume that, in some unknown way, you're warding men off. You feel condemned and confused.

Many married women don't know what to say either. They have never lived alone or made major decisions alone. And some make insensitive comments or suggest that perhaps you have the "gift of singleness." (We'll discuss this "gift" in a later chapter.)

Some assume you are on the hunt for a man and hold their husbands a little closer when you're around. Personally, I was blessed in my single years with many married friends who opened their hearts and homes to me and whose husbands treated me like a sister. But this is not the experience of every single woman.

Part of the problem is that family has become an idol in the church. Christians have reacted to the feminist movement's exaltation of career over family by doing the same thing in reverse— exalting family over everything else. Family is incredibly important, and the breakdown of marriage and family is the cause of many of our social ills. I do not think, however, that a married person is more important than a single person or that getting married makes you more spiritual or more special than a single person.

Now that I am married, I do not think my life is any more significant than it was when I was single. Of course, loving my husband and raising my sons to be men of God is incredibly important, but if you are single and you are walking in the call of God on your life, loving people, and investing in eternal souls, that is no less important than my calling as a wife and mom. God does not prefer me or love me more because I am married.

Moving Forward

If you are single, the goal for you right now is to figure out why you were created and move forward with a sense of purpose. The key word for you is focus. Identify the call of God and set your face like flint, pursuing Him and the purpose for which you were created. You won't intimidate your future husband; you won't scare him away. You won't miss him. Like an Olympic runner,

> IDENTIFY THE CALL OF GOD AND SET YOUR FACE LIKE FLINT, PURSUING HIM AND THE PURPOSE FOR WHICH YOU WERE CREATED

set your face on the finish line and refuse the distraction of what others are doing ("How come she gets a boyfriend?" "Why can't I have a man like that?"). Claim the truth that God is no respecter of persons and He has blessings in store for you, too—more than you can ask for or imagine—and move forward.

When you get married, your highest call will still be walking in the will of God—which will include being the best wife and the best mother you can be, but it will still include more.

If your life ends at the wedding altar, if you get married and just settle back and settle in, if you stop pursuing God and cease investing the talents He's given you, you will fall short of the purpose for which you were created. You will become stale. And your marriage will suffer.

When my husband and I were engaged, we asked several happily married couples what their secret was to a good marriage. One man said, "My wife is so interesting! I love to see her speak up front; I'm just so proud of her!" His wife is the director of a crisis pregnancy center who often speaks at churches and fundraisers. Their kids are grown and gone, and she has not settled into a humdrum life. She keeps growing, and he's discovering new dimensions of her. Her life stays current and fresh, and so his love for her is also current and fresh. She has a lovely home and makes plenty of time for her grandchildren, but there is another dimension to her life that blesses a lot of people.

Our lives should be moving, dynamic, and anointed, and that *can't* start when we get married; it has to start now.

Once you get a glimpse of the bigger picture, this will help focus your time and attention and give you purpose and goals other than catching a mate. By my late twenties, I realized that God was calling me to be a writer and speaker; He wanted to use my mouth and pen to communicate the truths of His Word and encourage people. This was confirmed when I spoke in my first conference overseas. I was

> OUR LIVES SHOULD BE MOVING, DYNAMIC, AND ANOINTED, AND THAT CAN'T START WHEN WE GET MARRIED; IT HAS TO START NOW

in Ghana, West Africa, at a women's conference, and as I stood at the podium ministering to hundreds of beautiful women, I felt like I had come home; this is what I was born to do! Similar to Eric Liddell in *Chariots of Fire*, I realized, "I feel God's pleasure when I [speak]."

I didn't know how opportunities would come, but I did know that those single years were prime time to invest in the talents God had given me. I had enough married friends to know that I had more time on my hands than they did. I knew that evenings free of distraction and quiet Saturday afternoons were a luxury and that I should invest some of those hours honing skills and pressing into God. I determined to be ready in season and out of season, and I spent many evenings with my Bible and my laptop open, praying, taking notes, and receiving revelation. I had purpose, and this guided my time and focused my heart.

If you have no idea what your destiny is, let me ask you this: What has God put in your hand? Like the boy with the fishes and loaves, if you offer even small things to God, He can multiply them and use them to feed multitudes. So, can you write, play an instrument, sing, organize, teach, cook, research, build, or sew?

> WHAT HAS GOD PUT IN YOUR HAND?... NOW IS THE TIME TO DISCOVER GIFTS... THE BEST IS YET TO COME

Now is the time to discover gifts, no matter how small, and begin to invest in them. Now is the time to ask the Father for a bigger picture of your life and for guidance on how to work toward it.

By the way, this is also true for my sisters in their "twilight years" or who are single again after being widowed or divorced. It's never too late to discover purpose. If you are retired and your kids are grown and gone, praise God! You still have time to dream a new dream. God still has another volume of your life written, and He's waiting for you to discover it. Don't shut down and assume the best is over. No, my sisters. The best is yet to come.

My only caveat is this: Don't limit God. Remember, a single man wrote half of the New Testament. God wants to use you to change history. Perhaps not world history, but at least the history of a child, a church, a community, a family, or an office. What He is calling you to is life-changing for someone somewhere, and it is vital that you discover it. Your mate will come alongside you and complement the work you are already doing. He will add to it and make it better, but there is much for you to do in the meantime.

As Israel Houghton sings, *"No limits! No boundaries!"*

Chapter 2

INGREDIENT #2: EMOTIONAL AND SPIRITUAL MATURITY

The next ingredient for contentment is emotional and spiritual maturity.

Let me preface this chapter by assuring you that you do not have to reach perfection before God will bring your husband along. There are plenty of women out there who married at twenty and were certainly not totally emotionally or spiritually mature. They were works in progress, just like you are. The truth is, there are lessons we all need to learn; we all need to mature. Sometimes God has us marry early as part of this process; we grow up with our mates and learn eternal lessons as married women. Other times, God keeps us single and wants us to learn these things before we get married. He wants us farther along in the process before He introduces us to our spouses. I have no idea why some women get one script and others get another. That's just the way it is, and we just have to trust God.

If you are single, take advantage of this time and get cleaned up *before* your man comes along. That way, you can hit the ground running and you won't have to spend the first years of your marriage wading through *stuff*. Deal with your *stuff* now, and the first years of marriage will be a piece of cake. Also, remember that like attracts like. If you are whole and healthy, you will attract a whole, healthy guy. Be the kind of person you want to marry. If you don't want a guy with all kinds of issues, deal with your issues so that he doesn't have to deal with yours either.

> DEAL WITH YOUR STUFF NOW, AND THE FIRST YEARS OF MARRIAGE WILL BE A PIECE OF CAKE

There are probably hundreds of ingredients to emotional and spiritual maturity, but I'm going to focus on just five. If God gives you others to work on, by all means, do it!

1. Deal With Your Past

We all need to deal with past hurts, childhood wounds, failed relationships, past abuse, and past failures. And as women, many of us especially need to deal with our "father issues."

So many women have father issues. Because of hurts and wounds from their dads, many women date the wrong men, give their bodies and hearts away too easily, fail to trust men, or can't submit to authority. The damage a bad father/daughter relationship does is profound. It is far better for you to identify and deal with your issues now. You will be more whole, you will have a more vibrant relationship with your Heavenly Father, and you will more likely choose a good man to marry.

Fathers are supposed to model the love of God for their children, albeit imperfectly. Your dad should be the first man you love, submit to, and respect. Every woman has an "emotional bucket" that needs to be filled by someone. If your parents fill it while you are young, you will be far happier and more secure as an adult. If you make it to adulthood with a half-filled bucket, you will look to someone else to finish filling it. God can and will make up for the lack and fill your bucket if you seek Him, but many women first look to men—and even other women— to meet their emotional needs.

> **EVERY WOMAN HAS AN "EMOTIONAL BUCKET" THAT NEEDS TO BE FILLED BY SOMEONE**

A good dad will love you unconditionally. He will affirm you. He will discipline you. He will fulfill your need to feel like a princess. He'll believe in you, protect you, help guide you, and provide for you. He won't do any of these things perfectly, because he is only a man, but you will experience a taste of all of these godly attributes from your dad. Then, when you are married, you will experience these same attributes through your husband, although, he too will demonstrate them imperfectly. God provides first a father and then a husband to give us glimpses of His masculine attributes.

My dad failed to model God's father heart in several ways. First, He did not provide for our family. He never found his vocational niche; he was in and out of jobs and unemployed for most of our growing up years. Thus, we lived with a lot of financial tension in our home and insecurity regarding provision. As a result, I've dealt with a lot of insecurity and a sense of vulnerability as an adult. I found it difficult to trust God to meet my needs. I constantly worried about money and found it difficult to be generous. This also fueled my desperation to be married, as I wanted a man to provide for me.

My dad was also a big talker who many times did not follow through on promises. He'd say things to make us excited about Christmas, and then on Christmas morning, he'd come up empty-handed. He frequently talked about the golden day when his ship would come in and we'd have plenty of money, but that day never came. As a result, I had a hard time trusting God to make good on His promises. I didn't know if He also would leave me empty-handed.

My dad also failed to protect us in many respects. Lots of kids picked fights with me, and I'd run home crying with a bloody lip or something of the sort. My dad, however, just yelled at me for not fighting back hard enough. Later on, I dated men who were inappropriate for me to date, and my dad didn't even try to intervene. He just wasn't there as a protective figure for his girls.

I had to forgive him for all of these things. I realized that he grew up in a fatherless home during a time when black men were told at every turn that they were subhuman. He made some poor choices and did the best he could. I cut him some slack, and God healed my heart. God also began showing me that where my dad had failed, He would never fail me. And slowly but surely, I learned to depend on my Heavenly Father to protect me, provide for me, and come through for me. And then I had to learn to trust my husband and not assume that he, too, would seriously fail me in some way. And I'm still learning. We are all works in progress.

My dad, however, *did* model some other wonderful godly attributes. First, my dad believed in me. All of my life I've had a deep sense that I could do anything I wanted. I've had a confidence that if I worked hard enough, I could do it. And I owe this largely to my dad.

Growing up, I studied piano seriously. I'd sit for hours listening to piano music and deep inside, I'd think, *I can do that.* And I did. I played some of the greatest piano pieces and performed in numerous recitals, and my dad attended some of them. He'd boast about me to friends. I could see his pride and his approval on his face, and I felt like I could fly. My dad's smile put wind in my sails and made my heart soar. Because of my dad, the sky was the limit. I could be President of the United States if I wanted to be.

> MY DAD'S SMILE PUT WIND IN MY SAILS AND MADE MY HEART SOAR

Everyone needs that approval and affirmation from someone. We need it from our parents; we need it from our dads. So many adults fear failure, lack confidence, and never fulfill their potential because they received constant criticism, rather than affirmation, from their fathers.

My dad also had many loving pet names for me. *Daffodil* was one. To this day, I love daffodils. Daffodils are a burst of bright yellow sunshine in the spring. By calling me that, he conveyed in a fun, endearing way that I was a source of sunshine to him.

> EVERYONE NEEDS THAT APPROVAL AND AFFIRMATION FROM SOMEONE

Lastly, my father provided important guidance at crucial times. Months before he died, he came to visit me, and as he was boarding the bus to go home, he turned to me and said, "Nicole, write." He knew in his heart that writing was a part of my destiny and that it was imperative that I just start. He had a prophetic insight into my life, and his words stuck. Almost every time I sit down to write, I think of my dad.

So what about you? Do you have father issues? Or were you blessed with a dad who loved, protected, affirmed, and provided for you? Because so many women grow up with dysfunctional fathers, they receive a double wounding: They aren't loved the way they need to be loved at home, and they don't learn to respect men. When they grow up, they go out looking for a man to make up for the love they lacked, and yet, they don't respect the men they date or marry. Often they settle for men who have the same or similar dysfunctional traits as their dads, and they fail to respect them the way men crave to be respected. They receive no love, and they give no respect. No relationship can thrive under these conditions.

Women need love, and men need respect. A relationship devoid of these ingredients *will* fail.

You owe it to yourself and to the men you date to deal with your father issues. Being healed of these realities will help pave the way to a healthier life and a more vibrant marriage.

Forgiveness

If you need to forgive your dad, do it now. But don't expect the wounds to be instantly healed and to feel instant love flowing through your heart. The devil will try to replay mental DVDs of your dad's imperfections over and over again. He will try to remind you at every turn of the ways your father hurt you and

> IF YOU NEED TO FORGIVE YOUR DAD, DO IT NOW

suggest that perhaps he doesn't deserve your forgiveness. But let me warn you; you must forgive. It is not a choice.

Jesus is very clear when He speaks of the necessity of forgiveness:

> *If you forgive those who sin against you, your heavenly Father will forgive you. But if you refuse to forgive others, your Father will not forgive your sins (Matthew 6:14–15).*

After making this statement about the importance of forgiveness, He told this very sobering parable:

Then Peter came to him and asked, "Lord, how often should I forgive someone who sins against me? Seven times?"

"No, not seven times," Jesus replied, "but seventy times seven! Therefore, the Kingdom of Heaven can be compared to a king who decided to bring his accounts up to date with servants who had borrowed money from him. In the process, one of his debtors was brought in who owed him millions of dollars. He couldn't pay, so his master ordered that he be sold—along with his wife, his children, and everything he owned—to pay the debt. But the man fell down before his master and begged him, 'Please, be patient with me, and I will pay it all.' Then his master was filled with pity for him, and he released him and forgave his debt. But when the man left the king, he went to a fellow servant who owed him a few thousand dollars. He grabbed him by the throat and demanded instant payment. His fellow servant fell down before him and begged for a little more time. 'Be patient with me, and I will pay it,' he pleaded. But his creditor wouldn't wait. He had the man arrested and put in prison until the debt could be paid in full. When some of the other servants saw this, they were very upset. They went to the king and told him everything that had happened. Then the king called in the man he had forgiven and said, 'You evil servant! I forgave you

that tremendous debt because you pleaded with me. Shouldn't you have mercy on your fellow servant, just as I had mercy on you?' Then the angry king sent the man to prison to be tortured until he had paid his entire debt. That's what my heavenly Father will do to you if you refuse to forgive your brothers and sisters from your heart" (Matthew 18:21–35).

Don't negotiate with unforgiveness. It will kill you.

When you forgive, pray out loud and release your dad. Ask God's forgiveness for holding onto bitterness all these years. And ask Him to tear out a root of bitterness. If you do not, this bitterness will be like a weed that chokes out any of the good, precious fruit that would otherwise grow in your life. It will choke growth, and it will choke joy.

Refuse the mental DVDs. Every time the devil tries to replay one, remind him that you've forgiven your dad, and

> **DON'T NEGOTIATE WITH UNFORGIVENESS. IT WILL KILL YOU**

pray a blessing over him (if he is still alive). Then move your mind to something pleasing to the Lord. Recite a Scripture; sing a worship song. Pray. Actively move your mind away from the bad and onto something good and godly. In time, your mind will be renewed, and you will actually *feel* forgiveness flowing through your veins.

Don't wait for the feelings. Do the right thing first; then the feelings will come. Lead with your will and your spirit, not with your feelings. Emotions can be like unruly children that need to be trained. Don't wait until you feel mushy feelings. Make a choice; then your emotions, like a dog on a leash, will heal to the will of God.

> And now, dear brothers and sisters, one final thing. Fix your thoughts on what is true, and honorable, and right, and pure, and lovely, and admirable. Think about things that are excellent and worthy of praise. Keep putting into practice all you learned and received from me— everything you heard from me and saw me doing. Then the God of peace will be with you (Philippians 4:8–9).

My sisters, this principle of forgiveness and mind renewal holds true for other issues as well. If an ex-husband or ex-boyfriend hurt you, you must forgive. If your mother wounded you, you must forgive. And you have to submit to the process of mind renewal. It is not easy. It takes work. But if you want true fellowship with your Heavenly Father, and if you want the righteousness, peace, and joy of the Kingdom, you have no choice but to forgive.

2. Deal with Other Issues

At various times in my life, God confronted me with areas of brokenness that needed to be prayed through, repented of, and severed. He showed me spiritual strongholds that needed to be cut in order for me to experience wholeness.

One time happened after my freshman year of college. While I was home for the summer, I asked a few good friends to pray through some things with me. During that time, I repented of a high school relationship that had ended but still plagued me. I repented for the impurity of that relationship and for making the guy an idol. The women praying for me and cut the soul ties that kept me bound to that person. I felt a difference right away.

Don't get me wrong; it took work to apprehend true freedom and wholeness. I can remember walking to the subway that same summer after the prayer time and Satan pummeling me with depressing thoughts regarding that relationship. "You'll never marry. You'll be alone your whole life. You'll never enjoy the embrace of a man." And then he'd play lustful videos in my head to make me feel really depressed. Sometimes I felt like I was going crazy! I'd walk along Eighth Avenue near my Brooklyn home rebuking the devil, reciting Scripture, talking to my soul, and reminding myself of the love of God. It was a war! The devil was mad that I had taken steps to be free, and he tried everything he could to put me back into bondage. But I won. By the grace of God, I won. Within months, the video tapes played less and less in my mind, and I thought of that relationship rarely. My hope was renewed and my thoughts more pure.

My sisters, freedom will take a fight, but God promises that you will win if you do not give up.

But thanks be to God, who always leads us in triumphal procession in Christ and through us spreads everywhere the fragrance of the knowledge of him (2 Corinthians 2:14 NIV).

Disturbing Patterns

Another time, God confronted me about a week before my husband started to pursue me. (God knew what was coming, and He had some more purging to do.)

> I KNEW SOMETHING WAS BROKEN INSIDE OF ME THAT COMPELLED ME TO REPEAT THE SAME PATTERNS AGAIN AND AGAIN

Over the course of about five years, I had had three relationships that looked hauntingly similar. I had chosen the same kinds of men and made the same kinds of mistakes in all three cases. After the third, I was afraid. I knew something was broken inside of me that compelled me to repeat the same patterns again and again. I didn't trust myself *not* to do it again. I felt out of control.

In all three cases, I had given my heart away prematurely, out of desperation, to guys whose interest faded within months. These guys too quickly became the center of my universe—before I even knew them! I just knew that they were Christians and that they liked me, and that's all it took for me to give my heart to them, even though they didn't even know if they wanted it.

Right away, I relied on them too heavily to fulfill me, and they soon began to back off. This left me feeling rejected—again and again. Attracting guys didn't seem to be the problem, but the ability to keep them alluded me. As a result, I felt inferior, and my self-esteem went from low to dangerously low.

Then, as they backed off, I began to see things I didn't like anyway, and I wondered how I had gotten in so deep so fast in the first place. If I had taken things slower, I would have seen that they weren't right for me, and though disappointed, I would not have been devastated. But when you give your heart to the wrong person, it is always devastating, and it always takes a long time to get it back. Sometimes the recovery time is actually longer than the actual relationship! So much precious time is lost and emotional energy wasted.

I felt like Paul. *Who will deliver me from this body of death?* (See Romans 7:24.) I needed deliverance, deliverance from whatever made me a prisoner of such dependency and desperation. And I was willing to do whatever it took to be free.

Do you see any disturbing patterns in your life? Are you willing to do whatever it takes to break them and be free? Can you say, "By any means necessary, Lord, untie me and make me whole"?

Once again, I gathered some friends who agreed to pray for me and ask God for prophetic insight into my soul. Once again, I cried a lot, repented, and renounced mindsets.

After that prayer time, I clearly heard the Lord say, "I don't want you to date, or even think about marriage, for six months." I easily said yes. I was tired of relationship drama. The Lord wanted to lead me on a journey of healing—of discovering His love, provision, and protection in a more tangible way. He wanted to truly be the Lover of my soul and teach me to find satisfaction and fulfillment in Him. *Then* I would be at a healthier place and more able to choose the right man. He also asked me to make a list of things to look for in a man, and He told me not to ever settle for anything less. I wound up with a list of eighteen character traits to wait for unequivocally. (You can see my list in the Appendix.)

Significantly, about a week later, Marvin Doyley came knocking on the door of my heart. We knew each other from church, and he asked me out for coffee. When I met him for coffee, I told him that God had told me not to date. His response? "OK, I'll wait." And during the next six months, we became true friends, and this friendship became the foundation of our marriage.

> HE WANTED TO TRULY BE THE LOVER OF MY SOUL AND TEACH ME TO FIND SATISFACTION AND FULFILLMENT IN HIM

The Master Surgeon

When the Holy Spirit puts His finger on something, deal with it. Don't run. Don't hide. Don't over-spiritualize. Don't say, "It's in Jesus' hands." What does that mean? No, my sister, you have to face it. Face the pain. Forgive, repent, renounce, cry, rage, and call others to pray for you. Do whatever it takes to be free.

Be like Jael in Judges 4 and put a stake through the temple of your enemy. Don't play with the devil. Make him suffer by commanding him to leave.

Look at family curses and destructive patterns. Was your dad passive, and now you keep ending up with passive men? Was your mom or dad emotionally abusive, and you keep ending up with abusive guys? Was there sexual abuse, and you have perverted addictions you can't seem to overcome? Did your mom have you out of wedlock, and now you have a fatherless child, too? Did your dad cheat, and your last five boyfriends were all cheaters?

There is no such thing as coincidence. If you prayerfully ask God to unveil any darkness, He will. He wants you free! He brought you forth from your mother's womb and invested you with life, and He has more for you than brokenness and regret. He has come so that you might have abundant life—not just-barely-getting-by life. Let the Master Surgeon operate on you. In the end, you will be more beautiful, and life will taste far sweeter than before you went under the spiritual knife.

Search me, O God, and know my heart; test me and know my anxious thoughts. See if there is any offensive way in me, and lead me in the way everlasting (Psalm 139:23–24).

3. Deal with God

God is sovereign. He is good. He is wise. He does all things well. He loves you. He has inscribed you on the palm of His hand. His ways are not your ways, and His thoughts are not your thoughts. He doesn't need your help; He is all-powerful and all-knowing. Rest in that. You must come to a place of fearing God, loving and worshiping Him no matter what. Say with Job, "Though You slay me, yet shall I hope in You!" (See Job 13:15.) "Though I never get married, though I live alone for the rest of my life, though I never have children, yet shall I hope in You."

> "THOUGH I NEVER GET MARRIED, THOUGH I LIVE ALONE FOR THE REST OF MY LIFE, THOUGH I NEVER HAVE CHILDREN, YET SHALL I HOPE IN YOU"

When King David's son took ill, David fasted and prayed that God would heal him, yet when he found out that his son had died, David bowed down, worshiped, and ate. He wanted his son to live, but at the end of the day, he acknowledged the sovereignty of God and knew that He was worthy of worship, even if his world had crumbled around him:

> *And the LORD struck the child that Uriah's wife bore to David, and it became ill. David therefore pleaded with God for the child, and David fasted and went in and lay all night on the ground. So the elders of his house arose and went to him, to raise him up from the ground. But*

*he would not, nor did he eat food with them. Then on
the seventh day it came to pass that the child died....
So David arose from the ground, washed and anointed
himself, and changed his clothes; and he went into the
house of the LORD and worshiped. Then he went to his
own house; and when he requested, they set food before
him, and he ate (2 Samuel 12:15–18, 20 NIV).*

Even if you believe in your heart of hearts that God has promised
you a husband, you have to be
able to hold that deep desire
before him with an open hand
and say, "But if You don't allow

CAN YOU WORSHIP WHILE YOU WAIT?

me to ever marry, I will love You anyway." Can you worship while
you wait? Do you love God more than your dream of marriage? Do
you subconsciously say to Him, "I'll only love You if You give me
what I want"? Or, "I'll only believe that You love me if You give me
what I want." How me-centered is your world? If Job could love
God despite such profound loss, can't you love Him even if He
doesn't give you a man?

You have to come to a point in your walk with God where you
love Him no matter what and you know His loving kindness and
tender mercies even if He doesn't give you exactly what you want.
Don't be a spoiled child; be a submitted, secure child who knows
how to rest in her Daddy's arms, convinced that He knows best.

To be honest, during my singleness, my revelation of this truth would come and go. Sometimes I experienced rest and at other times intense worry. But if you contend for this rest that comes only with submission, you will get closer than if you remain stubborn and unbending.

> *Surely I have calmed and quieted my soul, like a weaned child with his mother; like a weaned child is my soul within me (Psalm 131:2 NKJV).*

4. Deal with Spiritual Immaturity

Spiritual maturity also means the ability to wage your own warfare, petition you own judge, and travail for your own needs. (See Luke 18.) In truth, *you* are the one who has the most authority to lay hold of God's promises for *you*.

IN TRUTH, YOU ARE THE ONE WHO HAS THE MOST AUTHORITY TO LAY HOLD OF GOD'S PROMISES FOR YOU.

We can sometimes think we have to get prayer from someone more spiritual than we are—and sometimes it is good to get people praying and to receive strength and encouragement from brothers and sisters. But in the end, you can stand before God, bare your heart, and see His goodness in the land of the living (see Psalm 27:13). Yes, we need the humility to seek a friend or a pastor and ask for prayer when we're struggling, but we also need the ability to stand on our own two feet and help ourselves. Do you know how to speak to your own soul and encourage your own self in the Lord?

I remember going up for prayer one Sunday after the service. As I stood there waiting for someone to come and lay hands on me and pray, a voice said to me, "You should be praying for others by now rather than seeking prayer again and again for yourself." That was a small rebuke from the Lord. I had been saved a long time and knew in my head how to pray, how to do warfare, how to intercede. I knew it all but didn't do any of it. When I felt discouraged (which was often), I instantly went for help and had inadvertently trained myself to rely on other peoples' faith rather than my own.

> **DO YOU KNOW HOW TO SPEAK TO YOUR OWN SOUL AND ENCOURAGE YOUR OWN SELF IN THE LORD?**

That was the last time I went up for prayer for many years. After that, I began to learn to talk to my soul like David, *"Why are you cast down, O my soul? And why are you disquieted within me? Hope in God, for I shall yet praise Him for the help of His countenance"* (Psalm 42:5 NKJV). Even if you have the best spouse and friends in the world, there will be times when no one is around and the enemy of your soul will close in on you. At that moment, you'll either shrink back in fear, or you'll stand your ground and win your private war.

I believe every Christian who wants an abundant life has to learn how to get his or her needs met in God. We need people, but we need God more, and at the end of the day, He wants us dependent on Him alone.

I spent many Friday nights with the Lord, and many times I heard, "Turn off the TV and worship Me." I was discouraged and attempting to escape in mindless entertainment. The problem is, the movie, with its sex scenes or love scenes, only increased my discouragement. Nevertheless, it took willpower to turn it off and put on a worship CD or pick up my Bible. But I'm so glad for the times I did, as they built and strengthened an intimacy with the Lord that carried me through.

And the Holy Spirit still whispers at times, *Turn off the TV...Put down the book...Don't make that phone call now...I want to spend a little time with you.* My soul gets just as depleted as it did when I was single; the reasons are different, but I have found that Jesus truly is the center of my joy—not my husband, not my sons, but Jesus.

5. Deal with Yourself

I love the movie, *Diary of a Mad Black Woman.* It's one of my favorites, with its clear Christian messages and belly-laughing humor. But I also feel grateful for the insight into myself that the movie provided. I can relate to Helen, the heroine of the story. I watched it right after ending Relationship #3, and I saw in living color who I'd be without the Lord and the positive influences He put in my life.

In the beginning scenes, Helen seems to have a perfect life, but behind closed doors she is the quintessential desperate, passive, emotionally abused wife. She has a beautiful house and a rich husband, but Charles, her husband, often cheats on her, and after a while he makes no attempt to hide it. And she puts up with it—until he kicks her out of the house! She's attractive and smart but has so little self-esteem and self-respect that she allows herself to be walked over by a domineering, unloving man. She has no backbone, and he uses her and disrespects her. She was desperate to be loved and desperate not to be alone—so she settled for a man who didn't love her.

> **SHE WAS DESPERATE TO BE LOVED AND DESPERATE NOT TO BE ALONE—SO SHE SETTLED FOR A MAN WHO DIDN'T LOVE HER**

Unfortunately, I did that too. I am thankful that for me it was only in my dating relationships and not my marriage. God rescued me! But I can still remember those desperate feelings and those poor choices.

To make matters worse, Helen didn't, at first, recognize a good man when he came along. (The similarities are amazing; I also snubbed my husband at first. I had grown so accustomed to being treated badly that my gracious, kind husband failed to get my attention until sometime later.)

As I watched the movie, I realized that without God and the people in my life who helped me get a backbone, I'd probably be married to an abusive, unloving man who neither appreciated nor respected me. And I was so grateful for the dignity He instilled in me through the years, the boundaries I finally set in place out of self-respect, and the standard I finally raised.

As Christians, we tend not to think in terms of what we deserve and don't deserve. Well, sisters, you are daughters of the *King*! Don't settle for a man who doesn't treat you that way. It would be better to be single than to be with a man who treats you like a pauper. Now, I don't advocate a princess syndrome—you'll only eat at expensive restaurants; you'll only settle for expensive gifts; you'll only consider a guy with a six-figure salary and a Lexus. Give me a break. But I do think you should expect to be treated well, respected, and adored. Expect the guy to sacrifice, to pursue, to work to get you. Guys like a challenge. They'll go out with, sleep with, and even marry easy women. But they won't cherish them. You want to be cherished.

> **IT WOULD BE BETTER TO BE SINGLE THAN TO BE WITH A MAN WHO TREATS YOU LIKE A PAUPER**

God started working on my self-esteem after college. He taught me to like the way I looked. I had spent my whole adolescence feeling ugly, wishing I looked like someone else. And in the season of my early to mid twenties, He taught me to look in the mirror and smile. Oh, I still have bad hair days, but in general, I have learned to like my features and accept the way the Potter made me.

Nevertheless, for some reason, I didn't feel lovable. I still didn't feel like a man would really want me. I always assumed that once a guy got to know me, he'd turn tail and run. I felt attractive, but not lovely. And sure enough, several guys approached out of initial attraction, but within months, they began to back off and the relationship fizzled down to nothing but heartache and frustration—finally ending in defeat and turmoil.

Finally, I heard the Holy Spirit whisper, "You deserve better." He instructed me to make that list, to define a man worth waiting for, and then to be content and enjoy life until he came along. No more settling. I had dignity, true dignity, for the first time in my life.

Deal with your self-esteem. Learn to see yourself as a princess who is humble, but royal nonetheless. Learn to feel romanced by the Lord and cherished by your Heavenly Father. This way, when a man comes along, you won't settle.

> **LEARN TO SEE YOURSELF AS A PRINCESS WHO IS HUMBLE, BUT ROYAL NONETHELESS**

Your single years are also the perfect time to face and deal with addictions. When you're single, it's easy to make excuses for sinful habits; if you can't have a man, you think that you at least deserve a few fleshy perks. So you regularly visit porn sites on rainy nights. Or you indulge in sexual fantasies. You overeat even though you're already overweight. Or you allow yourself a few too many drinks with the girls. Perhaps you indulge in nice, trashy, sexually provocative novels during summer break or listen to the raspy, sensual voice of your favorite singer on lonely Friday nights—even though it only causes you to act in the flesh. Maybe you secretly enjoy flirting with married men just to see if they will sit up and take notice.

The devil lies to you, telling you that you deserve this little sin and that when you marry, you won't be tempted to do it anymore. You almost make it God's fault: "Lord, if You only gave me a man, I wouldn't have to do this anymore...." You make yourself a victim of sin instead of behaving like an overcomer. The truth is that if you make yourself a slave to a habit, you will remain a slave to that habit even *after* you marry.

> **THE TRUTH IS THAT IF YOU MAKE YOURSELF A SLAVE TO A HABIT, YOU WILL REMAIN A SLAVE TO THAT HABIT EVEN AFTER YOU MARRY**

That merciless master will not unchain you just because you have a ring. It may go into hiding for the first six months of your marriage, but before you know it, it will rear its ugly head, and you'll be indulging in that habit all over again. Only now the remorse will be greater, because you will be fantasizing about men other than your husband, or overeating to cope with the reality of kids, or trying to escape into some fantasy world when you should be building your home. You now run the risk of tearing down your home because of some habit you should have dealt with years ago. You haven't waited this long to be married only to damage it! Use these precious years to deal with the root of habits and taste victory.

I remember hearing a young married woman tell her story with tear filled eyes. When she was single, she often fantasized about random men she met. She'd meet someone in a store, for example, and then that night she'd indulge in sexual fantasies about him. The problem was, this continued even after she got married! She married a great guy, but she hadn't learned to control her mind when she was single and her mind still raged out of control even though she was now happily married. This resulted in great guilt and turmoil; she wondered if she should confess it to her husband or just keep struggling on her own. How sad!

Make no mistake, the devil is a tyrant.

All of us do things we are not proud of. Be honest with yourself and take a look at the things that keep cropping up and causing you to feel ashamed. Then let the Holy Spirit do His work. The benefits you reap will be well worth the work.

Chapter 3

INGREDIENT #3: A LIFE OF SERVICE

The Example of Ruth

One of the best stories of serving is found in the book of Ruth. In that book, Naomi and her husband, Elimelech, left Bethlehem during a time of famine to find food and wound up in Moab. Unfortunately, Elimelech died, leaving Naomi alone with her two sons and their Moabite wives. Then the two sons also died! Poor Naomi outlived her husband and her sons, a tragedy no woman wants to endure.

Naomi decided to return to her homeland. At least Bethlehem was familiar; perhaps she would find some solace there. Her daughters-in-law started the journey with her, but she stopped them and encouraged them to go back to their homes:

> *Go back, each of you, to your mother's home. May the Lord show kindness to you, as you have shown to your dead and to me. May the Lord grant that each of you will find rest in the home of another husband (Ruth 1:8–9 NIV).*

These Moabite women were still young and attractive. Surely they could find second husbands in Moab to take care of them and give them children. But if they went to Bethlehem, what chances would they have of finding men who would marry foreign women? They would surely remain single for the rest of their lives.

At first they both protested because they loved their mother-in-law; she was all they had! But Naomi prevailed upon them, and eventually Orpah chose Moab. She realized that Bethlehem looked bleak. Though she loved Naomi, her desire to be married and comfortable was greater than her affection for her mother-in-law, and she saw no way her desires could be fulfilled in a foreign land.

Orpah chose to find her life instead of losing it. She chose to "look after number one" rather than choosing a life of service.

But Ruth clung to Naomi and purposed to give her life away. Ruth risked life-long singleness (which in those days meant life-long poverty), but she gained Naomi's love and the God whom Naomi served. She chose Yahweh above her desires—and her comfort. Gleaning the fields was back-breaking, humbling labor, but she put God first and trusted Him with her life.

And look what the Lord did! Yes, she had to work the fields for a season (which probably felt like an eternity!), but her reward was Boaz—a far greater man than she would have found in Moab. In Boaz she found a godly, wealthy man who adored her and gave her children who would affect generations.

The way of Orpah is popular, reasonable, easier. I'm sure she got her husband. But any blessing she enjoyed paled in comparison to that of Ruth. God's ways are often initially harder, but they are always higher.

> **GOD'S WAYS ARE OFTEN INITIALLY HARDER, BUT THEY ARE ALWAYS HIGHER**

A Kindred Spirit

I can relate to that story. After graduating from college, I felt like God wanted me to stay in my college community and serve in my church; it is a small, rural area full of married people. It is not a great place for a young, single woman! Nevertheless, I obeyed the promptings of my heart, comforting myself with the thought that it would probably only be for a year, and then I could move on to bigger and better things.

Seventeen years later, I was still in that community and still single! Every year, I struggled with my decision to stay. Every year, I wondered if I had missed the boat and ruined any chance of ever marrying. But every year, I felt the same conviction to stay put. In many ways, those were wonderful years. I had wonderful friends and church family. After a while, I owned a home and traveled to beautiful countries—sometimes for ministry and sometimes for vacation. It was a very full life. It was also difficult, as I wondered often about the wisdom of remaining in such a small community. But God's ways are higher than our ways, and His thoughts are light years above our own.

In the end, when Marvin walked into the church, one of the things that caught his attention was my years of service at the church! He admired me for choosing ministry over a more typical career path and living in such a small community simply because God told me to.

My heart had always resonated with Ruth, and now I know why.

Serving Helps Us Discover Destiny

In reality, it is often in the context of serving that you discover your gifts and talents. As I covered in Chapter 1, the first ingredient to a fulfilled life is knowing you have a destiny and pursuing it, in other words, having a dream that focuses your time and energy. Some people do not know what that is. They don't have a dream, and they don't have purpose. The answer for them is simple: give.

As you give—even when it hurts—you will discover and eliminate possibilities. As you serve, people around you will see hints of the bigger picture and confirm thoughts and desires. If you want to find your life, lose it. Give it away; let it go.

> IF YOU WANT TO FIND YOUR LIFE, LOSE IT. GIVE IT AWAY; LET IT GO

It was in the context of serving at my local church that I realized my dream to write and speak—at home and abroad. If I had been driven by popular opinion and pride into a more prestigious, socially acceptable career, I would have experienced the good but not the best. I knew early on that I didn't want to just make money. I wanted something that captured my heart, and I found it as I answered phones and served someone else's vision.

Like Ruth, King David provides a powerful example of this truth. He did not get to be king until he served Saul for a season. Then God promoted him. Often we experience a season of serving someone else's vision before God releases us into our own.

Strategic Service

I write this with one caveat. While some singles struggle with selfishness and holding on to their lives, others run around serving all the time and never take time to discover what really makes their hearts soar. If you don't have a vision for your life, others will fill it with all kinds of activity that is good but not the best.

Unfortunately, Christians often guilt and manipulate people into serving them. We all know serving is good, and we all know sometimes God tells us to do things we really don't feel like doing. But if we allow the pressure to serve to rule our lives, we can easily get caught in an endless habit of serving other people so much that we don't take the time to invest in our own talents or to pray about the bigger picture of our lives. It's actually more comfortable to tackle someone else's to-do list than to come up with our own. We can get so caught up in performing tasks that we don't ever sit and dream.

By all means, serve. Serve in your church. Serve your friends. Serve at your workplace. But also take time to ask God why He created you. Read biographies and autobiographies, take those voice lessons you've thought about, take that course that intrigues you. Get that degree you need to go to the next level in your job. As you have purpose, you will have less time to give away; you will still serve, but it will be more strategic.

A wonderful example of this is our former babysitter, Mary. Mary was a college student studying biomedical engineering. She had a heavy course load because she believed God was calling her somewhere in the medical field, and she also happened to like engineering. Because she was a strong Christian with great leadership and organizational skills, she also served a campus Christian organization by mentoring younger students. Finally, she served at her church by babysitting for a few families—for free! (We didn't go to her church, but she just liked us. Praise God!) Because of her intense major, she could not babysit for everybody, but she chose two or three couples each season and enabled them to have date nights several times a month.

In this context, God re-introduced her to a childhood male friend. Sparks flew, and they are now married! I have no doubt that she will reap what she has sown, and one day when she has children of her own, she will have a babysitter as wonderful and faithful as she was to so many. She conceded to me that she learned so much about marriage as she served these couples—especially the value of date nights!

Mary had vision for her life, she invested in her gifts, and she gave away some of her time. God rewarded her faithfulness; He always rewards faithfulness.

> ## HE ALWAYS REWARDS FAITHFULNESS

I have seen singles who feel stuck in jobs they hate and spend every spare moment serving at the church. They have become passive, serving out of guilt. Life is happening to them. Rather than seizing the day, they let the day seize them and the years tick by. They are not happy, and they don't even feel called to serve in the ways they do. Their lives are busy and chaotic doing stuff, but they don't have any vision for their time. This is why it is so easy for other people to help themselves and use it for their own purposes.

The point is: Serving is good—in the right context and for the right reasons. Ask the Lord how you should serve, and let Him lead you. Then obey Him, unequivocally.

Why This Waste?

In conclusion, let's look at a well-known Scripture:

> *A woman came to [Jesus] having an alabaster flask of very costly fragrant oil, and she poured it on His head as He sat at the table. But when His disciples saw it, they were indignant, saying, "Why this waste?" (Matthew 26:7–8 NKJV).*

As you serve, you may be tempted to think that your life is being wasted. A voice inside taunts you, "You're wasting your life!" Or people around you say with scorn, "What a waste!"

It can happen for any number of reasons:

- You have a college degree and choose to leave your high paying job for the mission field. Your relatives respond, "Why this waste?"

- You decide to spend your Saturdays serving at a homeless shelter. Your peers see only the fun you could be having. But your heart is not in the party scene; it's with the poor. Friends don't understand it, but you feel tremendous joy when you're there. *Why this waste?*

- You're a talented musician, but instead of pursuing a career in the rat race music world, you serve as a worship leader in your small home church. *What a waste!*

- Instead of enjoying an early retirement and buying a sleek two-seater, you start taking in foster children, even after your own children are grown and gone. *What a waste!*

- Instead of retiring to the beach, you sell all and become full-time missionaries in a remote village with none of the comforts of home. *Tsk, tsk, tsk. Waste!*

Ironically, to most people, if you spend your twenties and thirties in prodigal living, that is not a waste as long as you make money and land dates. But if you spend those years serving the Lord and impacting lives, while perhaps making little money and staying celibate, to them, that is a waste!

When the woman in Matthew 26 poured the expensive perfume on Jesus, Jesus didn't think it was a waste. He thought it was a beautiful service, and He said she would be remembered and respected for it (while perhaps some of her critics would be forgotten).

Initially, many of the things God calls us to do seem like a waste. But is it waste, or is it worship? To worship means to give ourselves lavishly to the Lord, to love Him with abandon. The world, and even other Christians, might say we're wasting our lives, our resources, our youth—but really, we're just worshiping. We're pouring out our lives as a fragrant offering to the King of the universe. It's really not that strange.

> **INITIALLY, MANY OF THE THINGS GOD CALLS US TO DO SEEM LIKE A WASTE**

As I worked at my church all those years, I heard from every possible source: *You're wasting your life.* Strangers in supermarkets, college professors, pastors, saved and unsaved friends. At one point, about 90 percent of the people with whom I interacted thought I was pouring my life onto barren soil.

Only Jesus knows the big picture. His ways are not our ways, and His wisdom often appears foolish. From the beginning of time, God has asked His people to trod unique paths and do unusual things. You are no exception. God doesn't change. If He hasn't already, He will indeed soon ask you to choose the road less traveled and to look the fool—in a job choice, relationship, financial decision, or the way you spend some of your time. Follow Him, knowing that, in the end, God will honor you.

Chapter 4

INGREDIENT #4: BEING CONNECTED

S hortly after I started college, a church family "adopted" me into their family. They took seriously Psalm 68:6: *"God places the solitary in families"* (NKJV). They had me over for dinners, allowed me to sleep over when I was sick of dorm life, and helped me navigate classes that challenged my faith. As I spent time in their home, they demonstrated a healthy family and a strong marriage.

My friendship with them also cured me of a lot of selfishness. Many times I went over to dump out my woes only to be interrupted fifty times by their three year old. As my world was coming to an end, their daughter needed to be disciplined or comforted or instructed, and I had to wait! I soon learned that I wasn't the center of the universe after all, which was a crucial lesson for a young, self-focused college student.

After I graduated, that same family opened their home to me, and I lived with them for four years. And even after I moved out, for over twenty years I still joined them for many holiday dinners, picnics and family hikes. They helped shape me in many crucial ways; their love and influence was invaluable.

Another family extended an open invitation to me to join them for movies on Friday nights, and yet another opened their doors for me to hang out with them on Sunday afternoons. We went hiking, skiing, and tubing. They included me in all kinds of adventures. I have such fond memories of those times. Another family regularly opened their home to me for good southern cooking, holidays, and birthdays. Their kindness was palpable. And a dynamic couple, whose kids had already grown and left home, regularly invited me to spend the night and go for boat rides in Maine. There were countless walks, talks over tea, and coffee dates with married women, and afterward, I always felt encouraged and strengthened.

It takes a village to raise a child, and it took a village to help me grow up. I owe so much of my development as a Christian woman to the many saints who loved me through thick and thin. I wouldn't be who I am without them.

Single Friends Are Important Too

As for single friends, I lived in a household of four single women for ten years! When we moved in together, we all thought it was temporary and we'd be married within a year or two. Some of my original housemates did get married within a few years, but I wound up living there for ten years, while different women moved in and out. After a decade, I was a little tired of sharing a house and getting used to different housemates, and I was finally ready to live on my own. But looking back, I would not trade those housemate years for anything.

I knew that one of the snares of singlehood was selfishness. When you live alone, you can basically do what you want when you want, and you can become very inward and selfish. You can keep the house as clean or as messy as you want, and no one ever touches your things. You can also potentially get away with sin because no one sees what you're doing behind closed doors. I wanted accountability, and I wanted a degree of discomfort. I knew that sharing space and time would be good for my soul.

> **I KNEW THAT ONE OF THE SNARES OF SINGLEHOOD WAS SELFISHNESS**

Many times through the years, a housemate would want to talk when I didn't feel like talking, and this challenged my selfishness. Sometimes someone would leave dishes in the sink I had just emptied. Some of my things got used and broken, and sometimes my favorite snack got eaten. Each time, my flesh would die—which was a good thing!

As a household, we had regular house meetings designed for sharing concerns or issues that bothered us. I grew accustomed to speaking the truth in love, and I also got used to being lovingly criticized. A lot of prideful defensiveness died during those ten years. We were honest, and we challenged, encouraged, prayed, and fasted for each other. We learned transparency and greater financial responsibility.

We all grew up so much during that time. I even learned another level of hard physical work. The house was a large farmhouse, and it had an even larger lawn. None of us earned enough to hire a lawn keeper, so we took turns mowing. This was hard, tedious work. The house sat up on a grassy hill that took all kinds of tricky maneuvering to trim. It took a total of three hours each week, and we all dreaded it when it was our turn.

One hot summer day, as I was mowing, I almost started to cry when I looked at all that lay ahead. I felt like Ruth laboring in the fields, and I literally looked up to see if perhaps a Boaz was looking admiringly at me while I sweated. Nope. No Boaz. I wouldn't meet my Boaz for twelve more years. But I learned to work hard and be a team player, contributing to the common good. Those years felt like an eternity sometimes, but they taught all of us so many valuable lessons, and we also had a lot of fun! It was truly God-ordained.

In the end, those ten years also greatly helped my marriage. Our first year of marriage was a breeze! I didn't care about toothpaste caps being left off or toilet paper being hung the "wrong" way. I had lived with so many people and had become so much more flexible than I would have been. Neither of us was perfect, but we did not struggle with any of the classic newlywed issues because God had worked on both of us so much through our single years.

DECIDE TO OPEN UP YOUR LIFE AND BE CONNECTED TO OTHER PEOPLE ON A DEEP LEVEL

I am not saying that every single woman should have roommates or housemates. But I am saying that you need to deliberately make sure you do not become too self-absorbed. Decide to open up your life and be connected to other people on a deep level. Intentionally build relationships with peers as well as spiritual mothers and fathers.

You need a variety of influences in your life to become whole and stay whole, but it won't happen by itself. You have to work at it—and pray for it at times.

> YOU NEED A VARIETY OF INFLUENCES IN YOUR LIFE TO BECOME WHOLE AND STAY WHOLE, BUT IT WON'T HAPPEN BY ITSELF

For example, while I was in college, I prayed for a best friend, and God provided one. Similarly, a single friend of mine, who had lost both parents and a sibling, prayed for a spiritual mother, and God provided one. Having friends and spiritual mentors is a good thing, and God will provide them if we pray and take time to build those relationships.

Isolation is Dangerous

We're not made to go through life alone.

I don't believe in lone-ranger Christians. From the very beginning of time, God said, *"It is not good for man [or woman] to be alone"* (Genesis 2:18). I will discuss this in more depth later. Here I simply want to note that I believe this is referring to God's plan for marriage. After all, God did not create a best buddy, Steve, for Adam. He created a woman, a wife, Eve, for Adam! This is one of the reasons why singles can feel free to storm the gates of Heaven and beseech God for a mate.

He intends most people to be married, and if we desire that, we should not grow passive or apathetic but should state our case regularly, even as the persistent widow in Luke 18. However, this is not the only relationship we are meant to have. After Eve came on the scene, soon there were children—and then tribes and communities. As human beings, we have a great capacity for relationships, both with God and with people, and we will ever be incomplete without them.

Unfortunately, many single people choose to isolate themselves. They surround themselves with only one kind of friend (only guy friends, or female friends, or married friends). Or they have no true friends at all. They may have acquaintances—people with whom they chat on a superficial level—but they have no one in their lives with whom they are transparent, real, honest, and open. No one really knows them.

> "A MAN WHO ISOLATES HIMSELF SEEKS HIS OWN DESIRE AND RAGES AGAINST WISE JUDGMENT"

This can happen for many reasons, including past hurts and disappointments, pride, or the belief that you don't need other people. I call that last one the "just Jesus and me" mentality. Yet the Bible is unequivocal about this: *"A man who isolates himself seeks his own desire and rages against wise judgment"* (Proverbs 18:1 NKJV).

Isolated men and women become selfish, inward looking, and (frankly) socially inept. It takes humility to make friends and selflessness to keep them. Friends call at the wrong times; they have tragedies that we would rather not deal with; they need us when we don't feel particularly giving. Human

> IT TAKES HUMILITY TO MAKE FRIENDS AND SELFLESSNESS TO KEEP THEM

relationships are messy, but they are worth it. God calls us to love our neighbors as ourselves, and that often requires death to self. If we are willing to embrace this dying, though, we will reap what we sow. If we lay down our lives for others, others will do the same for us.

People are social, relational creatures. That's how God made us, and we do better when we are connected to others. However, sadly, some singles are isolated against their choice. This happens when Christian families have a *Little House on the Prairie* mentality, circling the wagons and trying to create a perfect world insulated from other people's problems. Mom, dad, and kids form a tight circle that consumes all of their time, energy, and money. After all the soccer practices, ballet lessons, and church meetings, there is little time or energy left to reach out to other people. In this sort of culture, single people feel like they are on the outside looking in, wishing that they too had a wagon to circle.

This *nuclear* family concept that crept into Western culture is not all good. In the past, parents, children, grandparents, aunties, uncles, and close friends all lived in closer community. Parents had "built in" help with their children because Aunt Suzy lived around the block, and Aunt Suzy always had a place to go for the holidays and Sunday dinners. The extended family takes care of a lot of loneliness and selfishness. Children serve grandparents, which staves off some of the self-centeredness to which they are so prone, and grandparents and single relatives benefit from the life and dynamism of children. In healthy families, it is a win-win situation.

> **THE EXTENDED FAMILY TAKES CARE OF A LOT OF LONELINESS AND SELFISHNESS**

But today we are so scattered. Grandparents and aunts live in different states; couples fail to reach out to singles because they are too busy or don't see the value of it, and single people work long hours, work out alone at the gym, and watch movies alone in their homes. Some alone time is good and necessary, but being alone all the time is good for no one. Every Christian should purposefully reach out to both singles and families and invest in genuine, lasting relationships. That's Kingdom living.

If you are not connected to healthy families and other single people, begin to ask God to give you those friendships. Keep your eyes and ears open. The Holy Spirit will highlight people to you.

They will just stand out, and you will want to know them. When this happens, be bold. There's nothing wrong with approaching someone and saying, "I'd like to get to know you; can we have coffee sometime?"

Of course, you must also decide to reject rejection. If a person you approach doesn't jump at the chance to know you, don't take it personally. Keep praying and keep fishing until someone bites. God has family for you. If your aloneness persists for more than a year, begin to ask God if you are in the right place. Talk to your pastor about it and be open to suggestions he or she may have.

Ultimately, community is so important that it may require you to move to find it. Of course, you should exhaust all other possibilities first. You don't want to become a nomad, continually moving around and looking for the perfect world. Roots are important. That being said, one of the litmus tests for whether you're rooted in the right place is whether or not people know you. A friend of mine likes to say, you know you're in the right place if "people know your name and they're glad you came." Do people celebrate you where you are? Or are you nameless and faceless? If the former is true, stay put until God makes it abundantly clear to move. If the later is true, God may have a different location for you. Just ask Him, and He'll make that abundantly clear, too.

Chapter 5

INGREDIENT #5: ENJOYING LIFE

A re you living or just surviving? I think a lot of women—married and single alike—are merely surviving rather than enjoying the abundant life Jesus promises us (see John 10:10). Are you just holding on by a thread, waiting for a man to come and rescue you from boredom and purposelessness? Or are you out there, determined to suck the marrow out of life now?

Single women, *now* is the time to learn to live! Don't think you can't start living until you're married. God wants you to live now. Who knows, it may just be that while you're enjoying life, you're husband will come along and find your *joie de vivre** intoxicating.

> **SINGLE WOMEN, NOW IS THE TIME TO LEARN TO LIVE!**

I read some great advice when I was single: "Live in such a way that married women are jealous of you." The message wasn't that married women shouldn't be married but that single women should live in such a way that married women wish they too had made the

---

*   *Joy of life.*

most of their single years.

Those words really screwed my head on straight at a crucial time. I had spent many years being jealous of all my married friends— convinced that the grass was greener on their side, sure that their lives were a billion times better than mine and that they had all the blessing and I had all the curses! But when I read that advice, I thought, *Is it possible for me to have such a good life that married friends look longingly at my experiences, rather than vise versa?*

I decided to take the challenge. It suddenly occurred to me that I could have fun, too. A lot of fun. It helped that God had blessed me with a wonderful friend—another single woman just a few years older than me who had (and still has) an adventurous, spontaneous spirit. Theresa now lives in Florida and, although a thousand miles separate us, we are like sisters. There is nothing I can't tell her; we've been thick as thieves through many, many ups and downs. We've cried with each other through tragedies and celebrated together in triumphs. How blessed it is to have such a friend!

At various times throughout my single years, Theresa called me and said, "Want to go to Paris this year?" "I found a great package deal to Mexico. Want to go?" "Nicole, you need to go on a cruise; let's save and go later this year." We had many wonderful adventures together.

After the cruise, I came back to work, and a colleague said, "I'm jealous! You have so much fun!" She didn't mean this maliciously, and she loves her husband and wouldn't trade her marriage for the world. But she witnessed me having more fun than she had experienced as a single woman, and she wished that she, too, had embarked on a few more adventures before children came and responsibilities doubled. I smiled and thanked God.

I can just hear the excuses: *"But I don't have any money!"* The truth is, I didn't either! I worked full-time at a rural church and made relatively little, but that didn't stop me. I made some crucial decisions along the way. First, for much of my single life, my living expenses were very low. I lived with two different families, and after that, I shared a house with three other women. I did eventually buy a condominium, but not until my salary increased sufficiently enough to pay a mortgage and *still* do some fun things.

During some of the lean years, I picked up a part-time job caring for an elderly woman in her home on Saturday nights. I'd go, make her dinner, clean up, help her get ready for bed, and be on call in the night if she needed to make a bathroom trip. This was not easy work! I lost a lot of sleep on Saturday nights; I missed some fun times with friends, and I had to do some unpleasant things. But it was worth it for several reasons. For one, all of this woman's caregivers were Christians, and just days before she died, she accepted Jesus as her Savior. We all smile when we think of her in Heaven. I'm grateful to have been one of the witnesses in her life, testifying of God's goodness. For another, caring for her increased my patience and compassion, and I learned things from her years of experience. It's awesome to be around older people; we can receive so much from them! Last of all, the pay was good, and the extra money I earned helped me to go on some of those trips and enjoy some of the finer things of life.

Ladies, if you are living hand-to-mouth, consider ways to make more money. If you have no money left after tithing and paying your bills, ask God to show you how to earn more. The Bible says,

> **LADIES, IF YOU ARE LIVING HAND-TO-MOUTH, CONSIDER WAYS TO MAKE MORE MONEY**

"...*it is He* [God] *who gives you power to get wealth*" (Deuteronomy 8:18 NKJV). God will help you find ways to make money. Of course, even with the extra dollars I made, I still had to save, sometimes for a year, for a trip with my friend. Living this way takes discipline, too. But all of the sacrifice was forgotten when we were lying on the beach, reading good books, beholding gorgeous scenery, and soaking in the tropical sun.

Maybe you hate the beach. Discover what you do love. Whatever it is—whether it's backpacking in Europe, going on a safari in Africa, or some other wild adventure—do it! I am so glad I experienced so many things during my single years because now, with a husband and children, it is more difficult. We do enjoy family vacations, but it takes more planning and more saving because there are more people involved. (And there's no such thing as lying on a beach relaxing when you have two energetic boys!)

Another excuse that might be racing through your mind is, *"But I don't have anyone to go with!"* Theresa was (and continues to be) a tremendous blessing. She was also single, which meant that she had the freedom to go whenever she could. She had a good job and had the financial resources to travel; she had an adventurous spirit and was a great travel companion. We enjoyed the same things and had similar temperaments. What an awesome combination! I realize that not every single woman has a friend like this. As a matter of fact, the older you get the more likely it is that most or all of your friends are married—and they don't have the freedom to jaunt around the globe with you. Nevertheless, don't let this stop you!

First, you can pray for a friend like this. Chances are there are other single women in your church or community who would also love a travelling companion.

Second, you can travel in groups until your travelling friend comes along. I recently met a single woman in her forties who had just returned from Thailand. She had always been curious about that part of the world, so she did her homework and went! She found a tour company that planned all the activities and told her how to prepare, and she waited until they offered a great package deal. Then she saved her money, made payments each month, and finally went! She met other women on the tour and said it was an awesome experience.

Another single friend of mind, who is in her fifties, recently went to South Africa. T. D. Jakes was ministering there and invited a group of people to go with him. She decided to go! At first she didn't know another soul, but she met other people in the group with whom she shared meals and joined for sightseeing excursions.

Sisters, where there's a will, there's a way. If you don't have a Theresa in your life, go with a tour company or invite your niece or grandmother to go. A married friend might even be able to go—especially if her kids are older and her husband doesn't mind. Just go! Your life will never be the same.

Of course, I'm not just talking about fun vacations. I also got to travel all over the world for ministry and missions. I saw God move in Africa, China, and the Caribbean. Sitting and talking with Ghanaian or Nigerian or Kenyan or Sierra Leonean women changed my life. Hanging out with Chinese students in Beijing expanded my heart and mind. The words of various speakers at a Trinidadian conference still resonate in my mind twenty years later. God blessed me with amazing opportunities to travel, and I witnessed with my own eyes the love of God touching people in many nations of the earth.

Sometimes I was invited to go with a mission team. Other times, I had to initiate the trip. For example, one day I heard a radio advertisement about an organization that trained people to teach English as a second language in countries that were closed to missionaries. The idea was that you would go to these countries to teach English while at the same time living as a Christian there. When I heard the ad, a friend who was in the room with me said,

"You should go!"

I felt something stir in my heart, so I researched it and wound up going to China one summer with a team of six other women to teach college students English. As a result, we saw several students and administrators give their lives to the Lord, and I made some wonderful friends. It was awesome! I still have such wonderful memories of that trip, and China is still dear to my heart.

Now that I am a wife and mother, my traveling days are not over, but believe me, with small children and a husband, it is not as easy. Now we're looking at four tickets to Africa, which is four times the cost. God can do anything, and I'm looking forward to traveling with my family. However, I'm so glad I made the most of every

> **IF IT'S NOT SINFUL, ENJOY IT NOW! TAKE THAT TRIP. BUY THAT HOUSE. TAKE THOSE LESSONS. DON'T PUT LIFE ON HOLD UNTIL YOU'RE MARRIED**

opportunity while I was single. My single sisters, do it now! Take advantage of your freedom and suck all you can out of your single years. Be careful that you don't subconsciously think, I'll wait until I get married to do that. Do it now! If it's not sinful, enjoy it now! Take that trip. Buy that house. Take those lessons. Don't put life on hold until you're married. When you're married, you will have a whole new set of responsibilities and limitations to deal with. Don't let your life stagnate just because you have not yet found Mr. Right.

Fortunately, not all fun activities cost a lot of money. I spent countless Friday nights watching movies, ordering pizza, and chatting about life at a friend's house. I took day trips to Boston with friends to do a little shopping and take in a show. I spent scores of Sunday afternoons hiking, tubing, skiing, and sledding with a dear couple who opened their home and lives to me.

God taught me how to love life.

For you it might include taking pottery lessons or guitar lessons or training for a marathon or volunteering at a homeless shelter. All of these things are harder to do when you have children. Dig deep and discover who you are. What makes you happy? What makes you tick? Don't wait for a man to define that for you, because he might make you into somebody you are not. And good men like women who already know who they are. Don't be mousy and indecisive. Be a woman who knows what she likes, who knows what she wants, and who goes after it!

> BE A WOMAN WHO KNOWS WHAT SHE LIKES, WHO KNOWS WHAT SHE WANTS, AND WHO GOES AFTER IT!

Purpose Brings Joy

Another aspect of loving life is having that dream I spoke about in Chapter 1. Having a sense of purpose puts wind in your sails like nothing else, not even a husband. As I stated earlier, your passions will help direct your time, resources, and thoughts. Even if you are in a dead-end job, you can love your life if you have something on the side that motivates and inspires you. You may not like what you do 9–5, Monday through Friday, but you love tutoring those international kids on Saturday mornings, helping them to learn English. You may wait tables to pay your bills, but whenever you can, you put paint to canvas and create artistic masterpieces that warm and astound people. Having vision for your life will help you to love life more than a thousand fun times with friends.

Are your married friends a little envious when you talk about your adventures? Do they listen longingly to your stories? Be a fruitful vine, thick with life, beautiful and green. Let your life be lush and inviting. I'm not saying you won't still have struggles, but let there also be delicious fruit and life abounding on the branches of your life.

Part 2

Dating with Wisdom

Chapter 6

THOSE PERSISTENT LONGINGS

In previous chapters, I discussed the reality that a person's life is about more than being married. Now, I want to make a statement that will initially seem contradictory: I believe the longing for intimate human companionship is second only to our longing for God, and most people will feel like something is missing until they find a life partner. Because of this, I believe it is God's will for most people to be married. He created us male and female to be joined together with one mate for a lifetime. That's how we're wired.

As I mentioned earlier, during my single years (and to this day), I had the closest friends one could want. I had married friends who invited me over for family dinners and movie nights. I had single friends with whom I had innumerable fun times. I had male friends who encouraged me and gave me brotherly advice and support. I had surrogate fathers and uncles, nieces and nephews, spiritual mothers and grandmothers. But none of these relationships filled the husband-shaped void in my life. The kind of physical intimacy, emotional vulnerability, and spiritual unity that I now enjoy with my husband can be shared with no other. My husband loves me unconditionally; he supports my dreams and has truckloads of patience. He's never jealous of me or catty, and he's not threatened by my successes. I can say anything to him. He's not God and he, like any other human being, has selfish moments and at times succumbs to his flesh, but our commitment to each other was sealed on our wedding night, and we wear rings as a sign of a divine covenant.

Why am I saying all of this? To depress you? No! I'm saying it to give you hope! The longings you feel are natural and God-given. They are not to be denied, buried, despised, shunned, or rejected. You cannot shake those stirrings in your soul. Don't let anyone tell you that perhaps you have the "gift of singleness." I don't believe in any such thing!

> THE LONGINGS YOU FEEL ARE NATURAL AND GOD-GIVEN. THEY ARE NOT TO BE DENIED, BURIED, DESPISED, SHUNNED, OR REJECTED

The Gift of Singleness

Usually people who say this are referring to Paul's injunction in 1 Corinthians 7 to remain single so that you can serve the Lord without distraction (see verses 32–34). But Paul also made it very clear that this is his opinion, not a command of the Lord. Paul had such a rich, fulfilling, and busy life that he had no time for a wife! He didn't long for the blessings of a wife; he didn't crave a woman's companionship. Neither was he burning with sexual passion. He was truly content being single. Marriage was not a desire of his heart. Other things gripped him, compelled him, and motivated him. For him, a wife would be in the way. This was Paul's unique perspective.

If you feel similarly, then stay single! Some people are completely satisfied with platonic companionship and intimacy with the Lord. They don't have a deep need to be a wife and mother. They'd rather bring the gospel to the African interior or spend their days in intercession rather than bringing Little Johnny to school and cooking meatloaf for the family. And that's awesome. If that is you, embrace it. There is nothing wrong with you. Decide to turn the world upside down for the Kingdom's sake. Be like Paul; be content and don't feel obligated to pursue the same goals as others around you. The man who wrote most of the New Testament was single, happily

> **DECIDE TO TURN THE WORLD UPSIDE DOWN FOR THE KINGDOM'S SAKE**

single! Don't shun the contentment you feel deep inside just because you live in a culture that idolizes romance. Stay the way you are and enjoy your freedom!

If this is not you, keep an honest heart before the Lord and keep praying until you get your answer. God might want you single right now to teach you some of the things we've discussed, but if you feel those relentless longings, keep pressing into the one who promises to give you the desires of your heart or cause those desires to fade if marriage is not His will. (See Psalm 37.)

Nothing Is Too Hard For God

I've seen too many single people give up in despair; it's easy to do! It's easy to look out on the landscape of single adults and see such slim pickings that you throw up your hands and say, "Forget it!" But since when is faith based on what we see? Isn't God able to create something out of nothing? Isn't He able to speak to the void and say, "Let there be…"? Isn't our faith all about the assurance of things hoped for and the evidence of things *unseen*? If God can cause Sarah, a ninety-year-old woman, to conceive or Mary, a fourteen-year-old virgin, to give birth, can He not bring you a mate? Is anything too hard for God?

> SINCE WHEN IS FAITH BASED ON WHAT WE SEE? ISN'T GOD ABLE TO CREATE SOMETHING OUT OF NOTHING?

I know the statistics. I've read them, rehearsed them, and cried over them. I know the ratio of single women to single men in the Church. I know the likelihood of getting married after you're forty. I know how many black men are in jail and how many men of all colors are gay. I know that many forty-year-old single men are divorced and looking for younger, cuter second wives.

These are the facts. But since when is the God of the universe bound by facts? Is your case the first one in history that leaves God wringing His hands in hopeless dismay? Do you think He shakes His head when He looks down and sees you in a kind of weary

> HOW BIG IS YOUR GOD?

perplexity? How big is your God?

If you've come to the place where you've decided you'll never marry, is this because God has spoken it to you and you feel peaceful contentment, or is it because you've given up? I am foolish enough to take Psalm 37 literally. If you delight yourself in the Lord, He will give you the desires of your heart. If your desires for a mate have been tried and tested, yet still abide as strongly and relentlessly as ever, don't assume a martyr's complex and decide that all those promises in Scripture must not apply to you. Claim them, yet again, as your own. And then, having done all, stand and wait for the Lord.

Jesus taught the parable of the persistent widow so that we might pray and *not* lose heart. (See Luke 18.) Sometimes we have to persist in prayer to the point of weariness. Then when we're too tired to pray, we need good friends to pray for us. But we cannot pray if we are double-minded. God desires truth in our inward parts. First, we have to tell ourselves the truth, and then we need to confess it to God.

Simply put, you want what humanity has wanted since the beginning of time: lifelong, intimate companionship. Don't let anyone convince you that this is unspiritual or that you should stop persisting, stop knocking, and stop requesting.

I won't lie to you; I think there are some serious problems in our culture. It's harder than it should be to get married. Many men and some women are too reluctant to marry, and both are getting sexual and emotional needs met through temporary relationships and illicit means. Spiritual needs are buried and forgotten. This makes it very difficult for those who are holding out for the best. These realities mean it won't be easy. Perhaps you'll need to fast, pray, and do spiritual warfare. Perhaps you'll need to ask friends to stop pestering you about being single and hold your arms up in prayer when you're tired. The good news is God is never bound by cultural trends. He is always able to bring forth beauty from ashes, and He delights to prove Himself faithful—in any situation.

> HE IS ALWAYS ABLE TO BRING FORTH BEAUTY FROM ASHES, AND HE DELIGHTS TO PROVE HIMSELF FAITHFUL—IN ANY SITUATION

If you are content being single, great! But if you are not, take the horns of the altar and don't let go until you see the goodness of the Lord in the land of the living. (See Psalm 27:13.)

Chapter 7

CHRISTIAN DATING AND COURTSHIP

In previous chapters, I discussed what you do when God says wait, how to spend your single years, and how to focus your time and prayer. Now we will tackle Christian courtship. Much has been written about Christian dating. Should you date or shouldn't you? What boundaries should you have? How do you get to know a guy without giving your heart away? How do you know if he's the One? I will answer these key questions in this chapter.

If you want to get married, you will have to date. I don't mean casual dating. That you can do without. But unless your marriage is arranged, you will need time to get to know a man who shows interest in you to discover if he is marriage material. That is what we call dating: spending time with a man who has romantic interest in you. For many, this process has led to excruciating heartache and oceans of tears.

> **THAT IS WHAT WE CALL DATING: SPENDING TIME WITH A MAN WHO HAS ROMANTIC INTEREST IN YOU**

This results in some questions: How are Christians supposed to navigate these rough waters? How are we supposed to get to know men without giving too much or too little? We know we're not supposed to sleep around, but how do we deal with sexual temptation, especially when we're in a relati onship? How far is too far before you're married? How do we have romantic courtships without compromising integrity?

> **HOW ARE WE SUPPOSED TO GET TO KNOW MEN WITHOUT GIVING TOO MUCH OR TOO LITTLE?**

In this chapter, I will share what God taught me about this subject. Like Paul said in 1 Corinthians 7, these are my opinions. Some of the principles are Bible-based, and some just come from my own experience and observation. So read, pray, and adopt whatever the Holy Spirit tells you to. You will be better off if you think about these things before Mr. Wonderful knocks on your door. Don't just "go with the flow," but be deliberate and circumspect. Your heart is too precious to treat in a cavalier manner. Be sober, but have fun!

Let me start with a fictitious story.

The Endless Interview

> *Jessica told everyone about the interview. This is what she had been praying for, hoping for, waiting for—an interview with a high-tech software company that would put her computer science degree to good use! The position sounded perfect on paper—and the pay and benefits were more than she'd ever dreamed of. Why,*

*she'd be making more than any of her peers; her days of
meager, frugal living would finally be over. She bought
her first power suit and made sure she looked perfect.
Then, that Monday morning, she left with plenty of time
to spare for her interview. She had done her homework
and researched the company well, and it showed. The
interview went perfectly, and she was sure the job was
hers. They even took her to lunch afterward and spent a
bundle on her meal. At the end, her potential boss, Mr.
Jones, shook her hand and said, "That was wonderful,
Jessica. You may be just the one for this position, but can
you come back in a week for a second interview?"*

*Jessica couldn't completely hide her disappointment, but
quickly regained hope and said, "Sure; I'll be here!"*

*When she got home, she called her family and friends,
giddy about the job. The next week, Jessica went back
for the second interview, and then a third, and then a
fourth. During one of the interviews, Mr. Jones even had
her do some programming—to prove her skills. And then
at the end of the day, he shook her hand, thanked her,
and asked her to come back for yet another interview.*

This went on for six months.

Six months later, Jessica went back for her twenty-fifth

interview, tired, discouraged, but managing to keep a modicum of hope alive. Over the past six months, Jessica had written a lot of software, had done some significant troubleshooting, and had become privy to many of the company's internal issues. She had also been wined and dined by the president, office manager, and several employees. They all had nothing but good to say about her, but they also never offered her the job.

At the end of that day, Mr. Jones took her out to the nicest restaurant ever, and at the meal's end, he got up and he shook her hand and said, "Thank you so much for these last six months, Jessica. They've been very fruitful, and we've enjoyed getting to know you. But I don't think you're the right person for the job. Have a nice day." And with that, he walked out of the restaurant and out of her life forever.

Six months of interviews and nothing to show for it! The company had gotten some nice perks, but she was left empty-handed. She consoled herself that she had learned a lot and had even made some new friends. And after a few weeks of mourning, she started her job search once again.

Soon she got called for an interview at another very promising company. She wondered why this company had been interviewing for years and still hadn't hired anyone for the position, but she chose hope, bought another new suit, and walked forth with regained confidence.

If that story really happened, most of us would think Jessica a fool. How could she let herself be strung along and used for six months, giving her expertise to the company and receiving nothing in return? The company benefited, but she did not. And yet, that's what modern dating looks like—and intelligent, capable men and women succumb to this system every day.

We comfort ourselves saying, "Well, I learned a lot." Or, "Well, we can still be friends…" But really, we're just trying to make ourselves feel better for wasting months—or years—of our lives.

There is a better way.

The truth is, men and women who go through these cycles of relationships again and again become damaged—not beyond repair, but wounded nevertheless. We lose some of our passion, our joy, and our love of life. Our hearts lose some of their luster as we give them away, only for them to be spurned again and again. We sacrifice some of our childlike innocence and receive, in return, a cynical, guarded

> **THE TRUTH IS, MEN AND WOMEN WHO GO THROUGH THESE CYCLES OF RELATIONSHIPS AGAIN AND AGAIN BECOME DAMAGED—NOT BEYOND REPAIR, BUT WOUNDED NEVERTHELESS**

demeanor that tarnishes our personalities and leaves us feeling robbed.

We are forced to become more and more detached in order to survive. We're told not to put too much of an emotional investment in new boyfriends or girlfriends—advice that denies who we inherently are as relational beings. Eventually, a layer of emotional residue clouds our true selves and makes it all the harder for the next person to really find out who we are.[1]

Believing that we can successfully guard our hearts from hurt through a maze of dating relationships is like believing seat belts save lives in airplane crashes. Telling people to go through relationship after relationship and suppress their emotions is like telling someone to eat without taste buds. It is inherently impossible.[2]

This is *not what God intends* for His sons and daughters!

Now, I'm going to drop a few bombs.

Bomb #1: Dating is a serious adult activity with a specific goal in mind: marriage.[3]

Like the interview, the goal is to discover whether you like the company, and if you do, you get hired! The goal is not to give perks with no long-term benefit.

The book of Proverbs talks a lot about the dangers of squandering one's wealth. But if you do squander it, chances are you can get it back. Plenty of Hollywood stars have lost their fortunes only to regain greater ones. (Will Smith comes to mind immediately.) However, you can never regain time. The years eaten by temporary relationships are wasted years. God is certainly redemptive, but something was lost (your teens, twenties, thirties; your innocence or virginity) that you can never get back.[4]

Today we settle for non-committed, open-ended relationships in which we give all (or almost all) emotionally and/or physically, only to break up and have nothing to show for it in the end. We tell ourselves that we learned something, but in the end, we've invested time in a relationship that has no future, and we've experienced a painful breakup that will take even more time to recover from.

Bomb #2: Do not date until you're ready to get married!

By *ready*, I mean mentally, emotionally, spiritually, and even financially ready. Let's look at each of these in more detail.

Mentally and Emotionally Ready

Are you ready to think about someone else, to put his needs above your own? Are you ready die to self on a daily basis? This is the reality of marriage and motherhood. If you marry the right man, he too will often die to self, but marriage and parenthood takes a profound amount of selflessness. Are you ready? Have you dealt with yourself, your past, and God, as we discussed in Chapter 2?

We all have baggage, but have you dealt with the things in your life that would make a marriage difficult? If you are overly insecure, you will be a jealous, suspicious wife. You will feel like a chain around your husband's neck. If you have a spirit of rejection, your husband will never be able to prove his love for you, which will create all kinds of headaches and heartaches in your marriage. As I said before, if you do what you can to fix these broken areas of your life, you will be more ready for a good marriage.

Spiritually Ready

Do you have a living, active relationship with God in which you regularly hear His voice and receive His guidance? Do you realize that only God can meet your deepest needs? Do you know how to access His presence? Can you hear Him convicting you, teaching you, and encouraging you? The Holy Spirit has convicted me of sin many times in my marriage. Often, in my quiet times, the Lord has whispered, "You disrespected your husband yesterday," or, "You should write a little love note today; you know how much he likes that." The Holy Spirit will be your best tutor and guide in your marriage; cultivate your listening ears now!

> CULTIVATE YOUR
> LISTENING EARS NOW!

Financially Ready

Can you support yourselves without working around the clock? I do not know how marriages survive when husbands and wives work opposite shifts and have different days off. I'm sure some do work, but it is not the best arrangement long term. Can you control your spending? Do you have a biblical perspective on debt, savings, and giving? I am not saying you have to be perfect in this area. Both my husband and I brought some debt into our marriage, but we were in agreement about paying it off and not adding to it. As a married couple, we've lived within our means. We have a checks and balances system with each other when it comes to money; we're transparent about how we spend and what we want to buy, and we hold each other accountable. Can you trust a man with money, or because of past hurts, do you have a need to control the checking account?

Bomb #3: Most of the things you need to know about a person you can discover through friendship.

You *do not need sex* to get to know a man; you don't even need to kiss him to discover if he is the One. As I shared earlier, about a week before my husband started to pursue me, God instructed me not to date for six months. I had come out of a series of relationships that took the same path. After the third, I said to the Lord, "I don't *ever* want to go through that again! I'd rather never marry than experience that kind of heartache again." After praying with some friends, I felt like the Lord wanted to lead me on a journey of healing and discovering His love, provision, and protection in a more tangible way.

Thus, as I mentioned previously, when my husband asked me

out for coffee, I agreed but told him, "I'd like to be friends, but God told me not to date for six months." He said he'd wait. Over the next six months, we did indeed build a friendship. There was no romance—no kissing, no expensive dinners, no gifts, no physical contact, no romantic words—nothing but a platonic friendship with plenty of boundaries.

During that time, I spent Friday nights and Saturdays with the Lord, reading, journaling, walking, and getting healed. Marvin and I purposely did *not* communicate every day so that we wouldn't become distracted or obsessive about the relationship. He respected what God was doing in my life and what God wanted to do in his life. He had only recently gotten saved, and he knew he needed to grow spiritually if he ever wanted to marry me and be the spiritual leader in our home. We talked a lot on the phone, and when we got together, it was in a group setting (barbecues at a friend's house, hiking trips with the singles group, and the like). We knew that if we spent a lot of time one-on-one, we'd slip into a more romantic relationship, and that was exactly what God had told me not to do.

During those six months, I was also checking off my list (see the Appendix). Each time Marvin and I interacted, God showed me one of those eighteen qualities, and when my list was finished, He showed me that Marvin possessed above and beyond what I had asked for or imagined. Scripture confirmed it, friends confirmed it, my heart confirmed it. After six months, I knew what I needed to know. We dated for a month, got engaged, and then got married four months later. *Suddenly God!*

What do I mean that we dated for a month? After six months of platonic friendship, we both knew we would marry, *and then* we allowed *some* level of romance into our relationship. In other words, we did *not* kiss, hold hands, or have candlelit dinners until we knew each other and we knew God's will. Once that was in place, we did enjoy some romance, but we kept it in check until our wedding day. Let me say this loud and clear: You do not need to kiss to get to know a man. That is a perk, but it is unnecessary and potentially detrimental until you know God's will.

Once we did kiss, our courtship moved very quickly so that the temptation for more physical intimacy would not overwhelm us. While we were courting, we had several friends checking up on us to make sure we were "behaving ourselves." I was almost forty years old, but I allowed women friends to ask me the hard questions. I did not resent this or feel like I was being treated like a child. I welcomed it because I knew sex before marriage could destroy the wonderful thing God was building between us.

Both Marvin and I wanted to honor God in our relationship; we were so grateful to God for bringing us together, and we felt like He was blessing us. We did not want to dishonor Him by disobeying one of His clear commands. We did not want to risk coming out from under His covering of protection and blessing by ignoring His Word on sex. We knew God would forgive us if we had sex, but we also knew that something would be lost that could never be recovered.

What we had was too precious, and we had waited too long to give into lust and potentially ruin our connection. We wanted our wedding night to be the first time we were intimate, and we didn't want anything to diminish the joy of it. And yet, like everyone else, we are human and weak. So we asked select friends to keep us accountable. And it worked.

Don't Give Your Lips Away

Why am I making such a big deal about kissing? Kissing is very intimate! When you kiss, you also give part of your heart away. Men can do things mechanically, but when we women give away our bodies, or part of our bodies, our hearts go along. A kiss is an intimate act, and a man does not deserve your kiss until he has proven himself to you. Don't give your kisses away for free. Reserve them for a man who has and is pursuing you, loving you, and convincing you. Make him work for your kiss and even your hand to hold. Don't do these things in a cavalier manner, thinking, *Well*, at least we're not sleeping together! The man who gets to kiss you has won a prize; treat your lips like a prize, not a pawn.

> **TREAT YOUR LIPS LIKE A PRIZE, NOT A PAWN**

The point is: Get to know a man before you let him kiss you. Keep your lips and everything else to yourself until it is very clear that God is leading you to marriage. And even then, be very careful. You are not married until you are married.

It is important to note that our friendship did not happen naturally. We had to set boundaries, like not communicating every day and keeping romance out until we knew God's plan. We deliberately withheld time and affection so that our hearts were not given away prematurely. It took God, the accountability of friends, and good old fashioned self-control to build a friendship, which was the cornerstone of our relationship. Any godly relationship will require the same.

Two Love Stories in the Bible

I will end with two stories of courtship in Scripture:

> *Then Isaac brought her into his mother Sarah's tent; and he took Rebekah and she became his wife, and he loved her. So Isaac was comforted after his mother's death (Genesis 24:67 NKJV).*

> *Now while he was still speaking with them, Rachel came with her father's sheep, for she was a shepherdess. And it came to pass, when Jacob saw Rachel the daughter of Laban his mother's brother, and the sheep of Laban his mother's brother, that Jacob went near and rolled the stone from the well's mouth, and watered the flock of Laban his mother's brother. Then Jacob kissed Rachel,*

> *and lifted up his voice and wept....Now Jacob loved Rachel; so he said, "I will serve you seven years for Rachel your younger daughter." And Laban said, "It is better that I give her to you than that I should give her to another man. Stay with me." So Jacob served seven years for Rachel, and they seemed only a few days to him because of the love he had for her (Genesis 29:9–11, 18–20 NKJV).*

The first story is that of Isaac and Rebekah. Isaac and his father, Abraham, realized it was time for Isaac to marry. So Abraham sent a servant to find a wife for his son. The servant, by divine wisdom, looked for and found certain character traits in Rebekah (for example, she had a kind, servant's heart). This was quickly confirmed, for as soon as Isaac saw her, he knew she was the One and married her without hesitation.

The second is of Jacob and Rachel. Jacob, too, knew he wanted Rachel the moment he saw her, but he was required by Rachel's father to wait seven years for her. He submitted to Laban's wishes and put his personal gratification on hold and waited patiently for her.

We can see a few key principles in these stories:

- Isaac knew when it was time to get married and he, and his father, did what it took to *find* a wife. He felt the need both physically and emotionally. Remember, there is only one righteous way to fulfill sexual needs and desires: through godly marriage. It is better to marry than to burn with passion (see 1 Corinthians 7:9). Today, too many men and women find sexual gratification outside of marriage, and this makes men, in particular, very casual about finding a wife.

The sex drive is supposed to help propel men and women to grow up and get serious about getting married.

> **REMEMBER, THERE IS ONLY ONE RIGHTEOUS WAY TO FULFILL SEXUAL NEEDS AND DESIRES: THROUGH GODLY MARRIAGE**

- Isaac (via his servant) had certain good, reasonable criteria for a spouse, and he didn't settle for second best.

- Once he found her, he took decisive action.

- Jacob was also decisive, but he was willing to wait for Rachel in order to do the right thing. In this way, he proved his love for her again and again. *Love waits.*

- Their courtship happened in the context of family. His access to her physically and emotionally was limited and guarded.[5]

Here are some further lessons we can learn from these passages.

First, Isaac *found* a wife. I believe that the man's job is to do the finding, pursuing, and convincing. *"He who finds a wife finds a good thing and receives favor from the Lord"* (Proverbs 18:22 NKJV). Women should pray for God to bring His best, and they should prepare themselves for marriage, but I believe pursuing is good for a man and waiting is good for a woman. It instills in each some very important character traits. It's important to note, too, that Isaac did not seek a sexual partner, a fun companion, or a date for Friday night; he sought a *wife*, and in her, he found all of those things plus more.

> THE MAN'S JOB IS TO DO THE FINDING, PURSUING, AND CONVINCING

Second, it's important for Christians to have standards beyond just finding another Christian. Friends and family will help us to know if our standards are unreasonable, but too often the opposite is the case. Too many Christians settle for a man or woman who simply goes to church on Sunday and avoids blatant sin. A good marriage takes a whole lot more than that!

Third, once you know you have met the right one, it is good to make your intentions known and not string one another along for years of dating and confusion. Some couples will need to wait to graduate or find a job to marry, but otherwise, there is usually no reason for a courtship to last longer than one or two years.

In today's world, most single adults live apart from their parents, so Jacob's courtship of Rachel at her family's home is hard to translate into a modern context. However, the fourth principle we can learn from these stories is simply this: Don't date in isolation. Do things in groups, where close, discerning friends and family members can "check him out" and confirm his character. Limit your time alone, especially while you're seeking God's will. Significant time alone and romance will only make God's plan harder to discern because your emotions (and lust) will potentially blind you from serious warning signs.

Fifth, you may believe that experience is the best teacher. Actually, the original saying is this: "Experience is a costly teacher; a fool learns by no other way." Some of you reading this will choose to date the modern way—for fun—and learn the truth the hard way. But my hope is that some of you will learn from my experiences and mistakes and spare yourselves months or years of heartache. Be a wise man or woman and don't have a stubborn heart. It is better to be alone on Friday night, while waiting for God's best, than to be heartbroken on Saturday, kicking yourself for wasting your time and squandering your gifts and talents on a company that has no intention of hiring.

> **IT IS BETTER TO BE ALONE ON FRIDAY NIGHT, WHILE WAITING FOR GOD'S BEST, THAN TO BE HEARTBROKEN ON SATURDAY**

Endnotes

1. Debbie Maken, Getting Serious About Getting Married (Wheaton, IL: Crossway Books, 2006), 148–149.

2. Ibid., 149.

3. Ibid., 150.

4. Ibid., 152.

5. Ibid., 159.

Chapter 8

HOW WILL YOU KNOW HE'S THE ONE?

John told them, "I baptize with water, but right here in the crowd is someone you do not recognize...." Then John testified, "I saw the Holy Spirit descending like a dove from heaven and resting upon him. I didn't know he was the one, but when God sent me to baptize with water, he told me, 'The one on whom you see the Spirit descend and rest is the one who will baptize with the Holy Spirit.' I saw this happen to Jesus, so I testify that he is the Chosen One of God" (John 1:26, 32–34).

A few months ago, I was talking to a single friend who asked, "So how do you know when you meet Mr. Right? And don't just say, 'Oh, you'll know!'" She was tired of the typical pat answer and wanted something more.

The following Sunday, our pastor preached from the above Bible passage, and I remembered the conversation with my friend. Jesus looked ordinary. He was right there in the crowd, looking average. John had waited his whole life for Jesus; he had anticipated His coming for years, and yet without the sign of the dove descending on Jesus, he would have missed Him because, to look at, there was nothing extraordinary about Him. He didn't have a sign on His forehead: I AM THE ONE. There were no bells or whistles, fireworks or heavenly hosts, but just an ordinary guy amidst a crowd who would ultimately do extraordinary things.

> **THERE WERE NO BELLS OR WHISTLES, FIREWORKS OR HEAVENLY HOSTS, BUT JUST AN ORDINARY GUY AMIDST A CROWD WHO WOULD ULTIMATELY DO EXTRAORDINARY THINGS**

I realized that something similar happens with single women, especially those who have been waiting for a long time. You daydream, you pray and fast, you talk with friends about the kind of man you'd like to marry. You don't know when he'll come, but you envision how you'll meet, what he'll be like, how he'll ask you out, and how he'll one day pop the question. You can build it up in your head so much that, before you know it, you have this fairytale romance going on in your mind that probably won't come to pass quite that way. Your future husband may be that ordinary Joe in the congregation, a few rows down, who doesn't really turn heads and certainly doesn't walk on water. He won't have a hallo, and Gabriel won't come and whisper in your ear, "He's *the One.*"

Most single women I meet have standards that are either too high or too low. Either they snub every man who shows interest in them because he's not spiritual enough, handsome enough, or rich enough, or he has some mortal *flaw.* Or they are so desperate they go out with any guy who has two legs and occasionally goes to church. When I was single, I fell into the latter category; because of low self-esteem, I went out with almost any guy who showed interest in me. But I've met many women who wouldn't go out with Jesus Himself, because, after all, he was just a carpenter. (And you'll never drive a Lexus being married to a *carpenter*!)

My concern with picky single women is that they'll miss a gem because he wears the wrong kind of jeans or carries a few extra pounds or doesn't have the books of the Bible memorized—backwards.

So how *do* you know? How will you recognize him when he comes? One of my favorite Broadway musicals is *Guys and Dolls*. I used to croon with the heroine, Sarah, "Suddenly I'll know, when my love comes along / I'll know, then and there..." Will you really know, suddenly, then and there?

As I've thought about my own romance with Marvin and those of some of my friends with happy marriages, I've come up with a few crucial things that go into the knowing—some signs, if you will, kind of like that dove resting on Jesus, to look for if you're getting serious about somebody and want to know if this might possibly be Mr. Right.

You'll notice that all of these points assume that you've spent some time getting to know each other. I know there are some successful instances of mutual love at first sight and quick courtships. But in general, I am a huge proponent of taking your time to get to know the guy. One of the reasons the divorce rate is so high among Christians is that Christians don't spend enough time getting to know each other. They are so afraid of falling into sexual sin that they rush the process and run to the altar. I totally believe, however, that you can date long enough to really get to know a guy and stay out of the sack.

As I've said, you must be wise, agree on boundaries, and have some method of accountability, but it's possible. We're human beings with the Holy Spirit resident on the inside, not animals during mating season! The purpose of dating is to get to know each other, not to see how far you can go without having sex. My rule of thumb is one to two years; this includes your initial friendship, the dating period, and your engagement. As I said, I know a couple of people who met and married a few months later, and they are still happily married. But this is the exception, not the rule.

> **THE PURPOSE OF DATING IS TO GET TO KNOW EACH OTHER, NOT TO SEE HOW FAR YOU CAN GO WITHOUT HAVING SEX**

Here are five things to look for in your relationship, if you are trying to discern if this guy is for keeps.

1. Respect

Do you respect his walk with the Lord? Whether he's a new

Christian or a preacher's kid who got saved when he was four, does he love the Word? Does he love to worship? Does he hear from God during his quiet times? Is he growing spiritually because he's teachable and humble?

Do you respect his work ethic? Whether he's a world-renowned surgeon or a telephone repairman, does he take his job seriously, giving it 100 percent when he's there? Is he respected and liked by his colleagues and co-workers? Does he have ambition to do better and go beyond where he is?

Do you respect his stewardship? Whether he owns a gorgeous home or rents a one bed-room apartment, does he take care of it? Is he a good steward of his money?

Does he respect you? Does he encourage you to dream and then do what it takes to realize your dreams? Does he invest time and/or money helping you to reach your goals? Does he listen to you, respect your opinions, and admit that sometimes you know more than he does? Is he proud of you? Does he like "showing you off" to his parents and friends?

> **DOES HE INVEST TIME AND/OR MONEY HELPING YOU TO REACH YOUR GOALS?**

Does he respect your body and take the lead in upholding the standards of purity you have set? Good guys struggle with sexual temptation. If he doesn't struggle, you should wonder. But good guys will also respect and love you enough to deny their flesh and wait.

Both men and women want to be loved, but even more than being loved, men want to be respected. If you don't respect him while you're dating him, you will never respect him when you are married. Do not marry a guy you do not respect.

> ## DO NOT MARRY A GUY YOU DO NOT RESPECT

2. Generosity and Sacrifice

Whether he earns $40,000 or $240,000 a year, does he make financial sacrifices to bless you? Does he pay the bill at the restaurant, surprise you with flowers, pick you up, and pay for the gas? I am not encouraging you to look for a Sugar Daddy, but I do believe that the amount a man is willing to sacrifice for his girlfriend is a crucial test. God asks husbands to lay down their lives for their wives—to literally die for them if necessary and to daily die to themselves to help their wives to thrive. If a guy can't buy you dinner when you're dating, he's not going to all of a sudden turn into a wonderfully giving husband who will get up in the middle of the night to attend to a sick child so that you can get some sleep. If he's selfish when you're dating him, he will be more selfish when you're married to him. Ladies, I do not mean that the guy should neglect his rent so that he can take you to a five star restaurant. That's bad stewardship. I do mean that dating you should cost him and it should hurt his wallet. He should be happy to deny himself his daily Starbucks or those new slick Bose speakers he's been looking at to bless your socks off on your birthday.

Does he drive the full way to pick you up, or does he routinely ask you to meet him halfway? Is he willing to hang out with your family and friends, even if it's a little awkward, because it's important and it makes you happy? (This goes both ways, but right now, we're talking about the guy.)

Look for the small and large sacrifices along the way. Good Christian husbands can attest that it takes a lot of sacrifice to make a marriage work. They die to themselves daily to be the servant leaders in their homes. You should see signs of this in your dating days. It will not magically appear after your honeymoon. Love gives, and if the guy doesn't give out of his time, energy, and money, he doesn't love you.

3. Approval from Those Who Love You Most

One of the reasons so many girls wind up with the wrong guy is that they date in a vacuum. In our modern culture, women go away to college and often settle down afterward in a city far from home. In those post college years, they start thinking about marriage. If they bring a guy home to meet their parents, it's often after they have given their hearts away and perhaps even their bodies. As a result, if the parents see any red flags, it's too late. In such cases, these women don't really want to hear what their parents have to say because their minds are already made up. They're marrying him; the thought of breaking up is just too painful, and seeking their parents' approval is more perfunctory than it is genuine.

The better way is to get your family and friends involved right away. As I've said, I believe the best way to date, especially in the initial stages, is within a group—going out to dinner with friends, going to movies with other couples, going to a friend's barbecue together, hanging out at your parents' home for dinner and a movie. In those initial months, when you like a guy, but you don't know what God is saying, it is best to date out in the open, doing group activities with those who know you and love you the most.

> IN THOSE INITIAL MONTHS, WHEN YOU LIKE A GUY, BUT YOU DON'T KNOW WHAT GOD IS SAYING, IT IS BEST TO DATE OUT IN THE OPEN, DOING GROUP ACTIVITIES WITH THOSE WHO KNOW YOU AND LOVE YOU THE MOST

I know, in some cases, you don't have parents or your parents live too far away to bring a boyfriend home for a casual dinner. What about your best friends and those closest to you in your church family? You want people who have your best interest in mind (and his too) to meet this guy—people who are not on Cloud 9 but who can see clearly and who have discernment. If it is possible for your parents to meet him in those early stages, don't discount their opinions, even if they are unsaved. Fathers have an uncanny sixth sense about men interested in their daughters. Yes, they can be too protective. But deep down inside, most fathers want to see their daughters happily married, and whether they are saved or not, they can smell a rat. My father always knew when boyfriends wouldn't stay around long. He just sensed their lack of serious interest. I wish he had lived long enough to meet Marvin and see a man truly loving me, but they'll meet in Heaven someday and have plenty to talk about!

You don't need to be alone all the time to get to know each other. The myth of dating is that you need hundreds of hours of one-on-one time, having intimate dinners, cuddling in each other's apartments, and enjoying romantic picnics together to get to know someone well enough. And you do need time alone, but not every day and every evening. The majority of time, especially when you first meet, should be with other people. A guy does not need unlimited access into your life and heart. Keep it simple, upbeat, and light by having other people around. That will help you to guard your heart, and those other people will be a source of confirmation of what God is saying.

After a while, when your friends and family offer an opinion, listen. The potential for self-delusion when you're dating is profound. *"Fools think their own way is right, but the wise listen to others"* (Proverbs 12:15). You may be a very level-headed, intelligent woman, but you can still become blind and stubborn when you really like a guy. Be humble and realize that better

> YOU NEED TO CONSTANTLY ASK YOURSELF AND OTHERS WHAT THEY SEE, AS WELL AS ASKING GOD TO GIVE YOU EYES TO SEE THE TRUTH

women than you have been deceived and married the wrong man. That's why it's so important for others who aren't emotionally invested in the guy to really check him out. You need to constantly ask yourself and others what they see, as well as asking God to give you eyes to see the truth.

You do not have to heed advice based in racism or other kinds of prejudice, but if someone close to you questions the guy's character or his true feeling for you, listen and respond wisely.

I remember struggling to let go of a guy who I knew probably wasn't right for me. I was talking with a good friend, and she simply said, "Nicole, he doesn't love you. I see it in his demeanor, his actions, and his words. Let him go!" I finally got it and was indeed finally able to end it.

4. Confirmation from God's Word

It's easy to deceive yourself and believe that God told you that this is the guy when it really is just you hoping and wishing that this is the guy. That's why it's dangerous to rely on this test alone, but it is important for you to try to hear from God and even to ask Him for a Scripture confirming His will.

As I got to know Marvin, I saw what a gem he was; he was passionate about God and heard from Him regularly; he had a great work ethic; he was humble, teachable, mature, and wise. In so many ways, he was too good to be true. But I did not have any "warm fuzzy" feelings for him at first, and that bothered me. On some level, it felt like my heart was numb. I liked him as a friend but didn't have those exciting romantic emotions yet. Those feelings are not the most important things, but they are important.

As I was praying about that one day, I asked God to do something in my heart if Marvin was indeed the right man. I didn't want to make a mistake and let a good thing go. In answer to my prayer, God led me to a Scripture: *"Don't judge by his appearance or height.... The Lord doesn't see things the way you see them. People judge by outward appearance, but the Lord looks at the heart"* (1 Samuel 16:7).

Through this verse, God spoke to my heart as clearly as day, "Don't worry about romantic feelings yet. Seek to know his heart, and everything else will fall into place." It felt like a thousand-pound weight had been taken from my shoulders. I asked God to show me Marvin's heart, and I fell in love with it. Soon enough, I fell in love with all of him. By the time we were engaged, I had all of those romantic, warm, fuzzy, heart-palpitating feelings. And today, my heart still leaps when he walks through the door. The Bible says, *"Do not awaken love before it's time"* (Song of Solomon 8:4). I think the Holy Spirit put my heart to sleep so that it would be easier to keep our relationship on a friendship level until it was time to move forward.

5. The Love Factor

So are you in love with him? Can you imagine life without him?

Do you want to be with him all the time? Do you love his company? Are you a better person, a better Christian, because of him? Can you serve God better with him or without him? Yes, all of those excited feelings should be there. And if he's the right guy, those feelings won't go away.

In conclusion, as I've said before, it's important to remember that all of this goes both ways. I have already started praying for my sons' wives. The thought of my sons marrying selfish, self-serving, immature women who don't truly love them breaks my heart. I am praying that God will spare them heartache and preserve them for good, godly women who will love God and love them with all of their hearts. Be the kind of person you'd like to marry.

Chapter 9

ONE LAST WORD ON SEX

Whenever a covenant was made in Scripture, the covenant-making parties sealed their agreement through the shedding of blood. One of my favorite examples of this is found in Genesis 15. There God made a covenant with Abram, promising him the land of Canaan:

> He also said to him, "I am the LORD, who brought you out of Ur of the Chaldeans to give you this land to take possession of it." But Abram said, "O Sovereign Lord, how can I know that I will gain possession of it?" So the LORD said to him, "Bring me a heifer, a goat and a ram, each three years old, along with a dove and a young pigeon." Abram brought all these to him, cut them in two and arranged the halves opposite each other; the birds, however, he did not cut in half. Then birds of prey came down on the carcasses, but Abram drove them away.... When the sun had set and darkness had fallen, a smoking firepot with a blazing torch appeared and passed between the pieces (Genesis 15:7–11, 17).

A covenant is literally "a solemn agreement that is binding on all parties," and in order to show the severity and the profundity of the vow, something had to die. It was as if the two parties were saying, "If I break this covenant, let what happened to this animal also happen to me."

Of course, the ultimate covenant in Scripture is that made between God and humanity, which required the death of His son. In this covenant, God promised to forgive our sins and cleanse us of all unrighteousness—forever—if we would but believe in Him. Jesus Himself shed His own blood to bind it and fulfill justice.

What does this have to do with sex? A lot, in fact. Marriage is a covenant between a man and a woman. On their wedding day, a man and woman make vows that they will be with each other until death parts them. They will be faithful to one another, and they will support, love, honor, and cherish one another above all others. Wow. Then they exchange rings, which serve as outward signs of this covenant. Wedding rings communicate to the world that this man has pledged himself to a woman and vise versa. They are no longer available; they are taken; they are one with someone, and they will never be joined with another.

When marriage is understood in this light, sex takes on a greater significance. The sex that happens on the wedding night consummates the marriage, and if the woman is a virgin, she will (usually) bleed. On that night, two people become one, physically and spiritually, and the blood is a sign of two things—that the woman has never given herself in that way to anybody else and that the covenant is now sealed between the husband and wife—forever.

This is why adultery is so tragic: whoever cheats breaks the covenant, and in God's eyes that is extremely serious. Covenants are never to be taken lightly; making a covenant is a solemn, life-changing act. And breaking a covenant, in Scripture, was often punishable by death.

The purpose of sex is to consummate a marriage, procreate, and help sustain the emotional, physical, and spiritual bond between a husband and wife. And because God is so good, He made it pleasurable. It is a blessing married people get to enjoy because they have made a lifelong commitment to each other. It is a privilege for those who have selflessly given themselves to another and daily do the sometimes hard work of sustaining a marriage relationship. It is a reward for being married, not a right for anyone who feels like having it.

Do you see why fornication makes such a mockery of God's original intent? Sex was never intended for those who have made no commitment to the other person. It was never intended to be enjoyed merely for the physical benefits with none of the emotional or spiritual ties. Sex is part of a life-long covenant made between two people who are in love, not two people "in lust" with each other who use it merely for the physical release. That's what dogs do. People have a higher calling.

Even if two people are genuinely in love, but have not made a

---
SEX COMES WITH COVENANT. IT'S THAT SIMPLE
---

lifelong commitment to one another before God and people, sex is inappropriate. Sex comes with covenant. It's that simple.

Let's look at a few Scriptures about premarital sex:

And He said, "What comes out of a man, that defiles a man. For from within, out of the heart of men, proceed evil thoughts, adulteries, fornications, murders..." (Mark 7:20–21 NKJV).

Now the works of the flesh are evident, which are: adultery, fornication, uncleanness, lewdness (Galatians 5:19 NKJV).

But fornication and all uncleanness or covetousness, let it not even be named among you, as is fitting for saints (Ephesians 5:3 NKJV).

Therefore put to death your members which are on the earth: fornication, uncleanness, passion, evil desire, and covetousness, which is idolatry. Because of these things the wrath of God is coming upon the sons of disobedience (Colossians 3:5–6 NKJV).

And finally:

You say, "Food was made for the stomach, and the stomach for food." (This is true, though someday God will do away with both of them.) But you can't say that our bodies were made for sexual immorality. They were made for the Lord, and the Lord cares about our bodies. Don't you realize that your bodies are actually parts of Christ? Should a man take his body, which is part of Christ, and join it to a prostitute? Never! And don't you realize that if a man joins himself to a prostitute, he becomes one body with her? For the Scriptures say, "The two are united into one." But the person who is joined to the Lord is one spirit with him.

Run from sexual sin! No other sin so clearly affects the body as this one does. For sexual immorality is a sin against your own body. Don't you realize that your body is the temple of the Holy Spirit, who lives in you and was given to you by God? You do not belong to yourself, for God bought you with a high price. So you must honor God with your body (1 Corinthians 6:13, 15–20).

This last passage is pretty clear. When you sleep with someone, you become one with that person. That's why it's so difficult to break up. When you have sex, your bodies and your spirits are intertwined, and breaking up feels like you're ripping something apart. It feels like a mini divorce! You've done a sacred act meant for those who have cut covenant, but you have no covenant! You've given something to a man that he doesn't deserve, since he's made no lifelong commitment to you. And you can never get it back. You've cheapened something divine for mere physical or emotional fulfillment, and in doing so, you've sinned against your own body, the very dwelling of the Holy Spirit.

Because of how we're wired, women feel this more profoundly. We feel the bond; we sense the profundity of the moment, and we don't want the guy to leave. Sex is the language of permanence, and we don't want the relationship to end. A soul tie has been created; that is, our souls are tied to a man through sex, and this makes it very difficult to break up. But then the guy leaves, or God makes it plain that we should break up, and we feel our hearts ripped in two. It's a kind of pain human beings weren't meant to endure. One man. One woman. One lifetime. That's the environment for sex— not multiple partners for physical thrills.

I know I'm coming down on this issue hard. And I know that we humans have a powerful sex drive. I've heard, particularly for men, that it is second only to the drive to stay alive. I am not belittling the yearnings and frustration of pent up passions. With the quantity of physical temptations surrounding us today, it is a wonder anyone can stay pure. Between internet pornography, television ads, magazine covers, talk shows, and a multitude of other venues, sex is "in our faces" all the time. But God promises we will not be tempted beyond what we can endure. He knows all about the twenty-first century media, and He still promises to sustain us and provide a way out of every temptation.

I struggled a lot with sexual purity. Many times I had to turn off the television because a sex scene came on that tormented me. I struggled with desires, and bedroom scenes only made life more difficult. I fought to keep my thoughts pure, and I reminded God many times of Paul's words, "It is better to marry than to burn"! I didn't do it all perfectly. But by God's grace and tender mercies, I did manage to stay out of the sack in my adult years, and my husband was so blessed that there were no sexual encounters in my recent memory.

One of the things that helped me to stay on the straight and narrow was a desire to have integrity while I served in ministry. During many of my single years, I led worship on Sunday mornings and sometimes taught sermons. I had enough fear of God to know that fornicating on Saturday and then getting up in the pulpit on Sunday would be a mockery. I had heard about leaders who led duel lives, and I didn't want to be one of them. If I wanted God's anointing, if I wanted His Spirit present while I was leading worship or teaching or even just living my life day-to-day, I couldn't flagrantly disobey a clear command.

I may have hidden it from human eyes, but God sees everything. He would know, and there would be consequences. I didn't want to lose His nearness for a moment. I felt desperate for His presence,

His approval, and His companionship, and I knew willful sin would put a wedge between us. He'd still love me, but He wouldn't approve of my actions, and that would sting. I wanted no part of it.

Sisters, His nearness is our *good*; don't sacrifice that for a man. If a man truly loves you, he will lead you closer to God, not farther away. You can have both intimacy with God and intimacy with a man, but only if you do things God's way and in God's time.

> YOU CAN HAVE BOTH INTIMACY WITH GOD AND INTIMACY WITH A MAN, BUT ONLY IF YOU DO THINGS GOD'S WAY AND IN GOD'S TIME

When my husband got saved, he turned off cable TV. As a new Christian man, he found it difficult to keep his mind pure with all the Victoria's Secret ads, the HBO movies, and everything else. So he quit cable, rented only PG-13 movies, read good books, and took guitar lessons. *"How can a young man keep his way pure? By living according to your word"* (Psalm 119:9).

How are you supposed to keep yourself pure for your marriage partner? *By any means necessary.* Jesus said,

> *If your right eye causes you to sin, gouge it out and throw it away. It is better for you to lose one part of your body than for your whole body to be thrown into hell. And if your right hand causes you to sin, cut it off and throw it away. It is better for you to lose one part of your body than for your whole body to go into hell (Matthew*

5:29–30).

I'm not advocating any gouging or cutting, but this passage makes it clear that you should take extreme measures, if necessary, to keep yourself from sin. In God's economy, it's worth it!

My sisters, save yourself for a man who promises to love you forever. Save your body for a man who has pursued you, wooed you, and proven himself to you. Save your passion for a

> LOVE WAITS. IF HE LOVES YOU, HE WILL WAIT

man who has committed himself to forsake all others. Give your body to him as a gift to be unwrapped on the wedding night. Love waits. If he loves you, he will wait.

When you are dating or engaged, do whatever it takes to stay out of bed. If kissing leads to too much passion, stop kissing. If being alone leads to intimate touching, don't spend a lot of time alone. This is why I said to keep physical contact to a minimum (or nonexistent) until God makes it abundantly clear that you will marry. And then, keep your engagement short.

Don't wear overly sexy clothing; don't rub up against your man and expect him to keep his hands to himself. Don't tease. Help him to stay pure, and he should also help you. Make it easier for him, not harder. As Solomon urges in Song of Solomon: *"Do not arouse or awaken love until it so desires"* (3:5 NKJV). Don't arouse sexual passion in your man until it can be righteously satisfied. When

Marvin and I were just friends, several times the Holy Spirit said, "Don't wear that." We would be seeing each other at a barbecue or something, and I wanted to wear something a little sexy. But God reminded me that we were just friends, and He told me to save the cute dresses for later.

I know couples who could not be alone during the final months of their engagement. The temptation was too great. So they ate out, took walks, hung out together with friends, and talked on the phone. Do whatever it takes to save sex for marriage.

Marvin and I gave each other a curfew. We soon learned that being alone in each other's houses after 10:00 P.M. led to too much temptation. After 10:00, we both started getting tired and losing self-control. So one of us, usually Marvin, would say, "It's time for me to go." Or, "It's time for you to go home." He took the lead in this, and I loved him all the more for it. Ladies, men can control themselves. They are not dogs. Wait for a man who loves you enough to control his passions.

> **WAIT FOR A MAN WHO LOVES YOU ENOUGH TO CONTROL HIS PASSIONS**

But what if you're not a virgin? Here's what God's Word says:

> *But if we confess our sins to him, he is faithful and just to forgive us our sins and to cleanse us from all wickedness (1 John 1:9).*

This Scripture is good news! Praise Him! If you've already been sexually active, confess it to the Father (if you haven't already), and then go and sin no more. You must also break the soul tie that was created in that sexual bond. Go before the Father and ask Him to break that bond. Ask Him to cleanse you and help you to release this man from your thoughts and desires. He will do this, but you must be yielded to Him and committed to purity.

God is ever a forgiver and a redeemer. If you confess and allow the Holy Spirit to cleanse you, you will have an awesome wedding night with your man and a great sex life as a married woman. Don't fret. There is no shame in the Kingdom. As a consequence of your sin, it may be harder for you to wait, but God will give you the strength. You can do it. No one ever died from abstinence. You need air, food, and water, but you do not need sex to live. It is a blessing you will enjoy in due time. Give that to the Lord too, and trust Him. He knows all about it.

Chapter 10

FINAL THOUGHTS

When I was single, several of my married friends said, "Enjoy your freedom!" At the time, I couldn't appreciate these words. I thought, *Yeah, yeah. Easy for you to say; you have your man!* Now I'm the one saying, "Enjoy your freedom!" My husband and I struggle to have time together and time alone to pray. On Saturdays, we often pass like ships in the night—one going on errands with the boys, another going to have a couple of hours alone before dinner. I was a busy single woman, but never was life the juggling act that it is now, and we only have two children!

You can't spend money the way you want or spend your Saturdays however the mood hits. Your body is not your own, your time is not your own, and your money is not your own. I'm not saying that you lose your identity, but you do die to yourself constantly. Motherhood in particular is a 24/7 job. There are many mornings when I have awakened and thought, *Can I take today off?* The answer is, of course, no. There is no such thing as a day off from motherhood.

I don't mean to paint a grim picture. I've stated earlier what a blessing marriage is, and children are a gift from the Lord. The inconvenience you experience pales in comparison to the love you feel. That love gives you the strength to endure the sleepless nights and rainy days inside with a fussy child.

The truth is, I rarely feel lonely anymore, and I do know a deep, deep satisfaction experiencing answered prayer on a daily basis. Since I was made to be married, I do feel more fulfilled as a married woman, and longing fulfilled is truly a tree of life. (See Proverbs 13:12.) But I feel just as desperate for God as I did ten years ago. Different things drive me to my knees, and tears flow for different reason, but they do flow.

Our need for God and for a deep intimacy with Him is something all women have in common, married or not. A husband will never, ever take the place of God. You draw near to Him now, and you will draw near to Him when you are married. Learn to access His presence now. Learn to worship and feel the Lover of your soul fill you up to overflowing. Pour your alabaster jar on the feet of Jesus (those things that are most precious to you—like your desire to be married). Let the fragrance fill the room. See the love in His eyes. Know His forgiveness and tenderness. Hear His approval. Let the Shepherd of your soul lead you to green pastures and sweet, refreshing waters. Allow Him to fill you and sustain you.

> OUR NEED FOR GOD AND FOR A DEEP INTIMACY WITH HIM IS SOMETHING ALL WOMEN HAVE IN COMMON, MARRIED OR NOT

And smile, my sister, smile. He has such good things in store for you—more than you can ask for or imagine. Live in contented expectancy.

Be still and know that I am God.

Appendix

A MAN WORTH WAITING FOR (MY LIST)

Sometimes people ask me about my list—that is, the list of traits I began to look for in the man I wanted to marry. As I shared earlier, I realized after break-up #3 that I had made the same error again and again: I had settled for a man who didn't really love me and didn't possess the qualities I valued anyway. God showed me that my standards were too low and that I didn't value myself enough to say no to dates with men who raised red flags. Indeed, the only thing I wanted to know was whether they liked me, and if they did, I went out with them, subconsciously assuming that I didn't deserve something more, someone better. Simply being noticed and liked in a non-committal, casual way was enough for me to throw my heart into the hands of a man who didn't want it and didn't deserve it.

So I share my list below, not so that you will carbon copy it as your own (you will value different things, and that's great) but so that you will begin to think about what you want in a man. Our current culture does not value high standards. There is a cynicism that says, "All men are dogs," or "Any man is better than no man," but as Christians, we have to stand opposed to such thinking and raise a godly standard. Good men *are* out there, and having no man really is better than having the wrong man! You can experience more fulfillment and vitality as a single woman than you will dating the wrong person.

What will the right man look like for you? Will you know him when you see him? Are you only looking for superficial, shallow qualities? Or will you only go out with Mr. Perfect (that is, the reincarnation of Jesus Himself)? Your man will not be perfect, so what will you settle for, and what will you demand?

As I stated in the chapter on dating, when Marvin and I were just friends, I measured him against this list and found that he had all eighteen characteristics, plus many things I hadn't even thought of! By the time we went out on our first date, I knew he was *the One*. I knew his heart before I ever kissed him, and I respected him before we even held hands. Knowing him preceded romance, and that made all the difference.

My List

1. Generous, kind, big hearted; generous with words, money, and time

I had dated one guy in particular who always wanted to "go Dutch"; we'd split the bill. I remember feeling common and a bit like I was doing him a favor by going out with him. He was tight with his money—when it came to spending it on me, anyway. At first, I gave him the benefit of the doubt because he was a graduate student, but then I saw him freely spending money on himself. This was one of the many ways in which I realized he didn't really love me—as there was little practical sacrifice on his part. Love gives. He also tightly guarded his time, meting out little bits to me here and there, like throwing a bone to a dog. And he rarely opened his heart to me. He rarely offered freely, on his own, "You're beautiful," or "I really like you." I had to squeeze such sentiments out of him. And the rest of the time, he held his cards close to his chest.

This trait created so much unhappiness and turmoil in my heart that I finally realized what I really wanted was the opposite. It also occurred to me that this was one of the positive traits my deceased father possessed. I spent a lot of years judging him for his faults and then, largely because of the men I dated, I saw that (all the bad aside) he had a big heart. He was different from my boyfriends. He laughed big, wept openly, and gave bear hugs and sloppy kisses. He was bad with money, but when he had it, he spent it generously on us. I missed that giving spirit and wanted it in my husband. So this trait easily claimed first place and became the sine quo non** of the next man I dated.

Marvin bought me a dozen multi-colored roses on our first date. He always picked me up, covered the bill, and came up with new things for us to do. He planned our dates and freely complimented me. All these were signs of a generous heart. He's an intuitive

---

** *without which nothing*

"heart guy"; in other words, he leads with his heart and isn't overly analytical. I loved that then and still do!

2. Has kind parents who love me and welcome me into their family

Since my father and all my grandparents had died, and all that remained was my sister, her family, and my mom, I had wistful thoughts of warm, cheerful Christmases with the in-laws and experiencing from my husband's father something of the paternal affection I earnestly missed. My family is so small, and I always wanted to taste the "big family" experience with aunties and babies and a wise, old granddad. In truth, what I lack in natural family, God has more than made up for in church family. I am rich with extraordinary friends. Nonetheless, the longing for blood family gatherings remained, and I took a risk and put this on my list. This was one of the traits I would be willing to do without, but it couldn't hurt to make my requests known to God and see if He might grant me this desire too.

Because Marvin's parents live in Jamaica, I didn't get to know them before our wedding, but since then, both his mom and dad have warmly embraced me. His mom stayed with us for a month when our second son was born, and we really bonded. She cooked for us and doted over her new grandson, and she always wants to talk to me when they call. Also, it is an added bonus to have relatives in the Caribbean!

3. Humble and teachable, able to say "I'm sorry," and eager to learn from others

4. Has good relationships in his life with male mentors, close male friends, and family

Numbers three and four both reveal a humble heart, one that is open, accessible, and soft. For some reason, in my earlier years I was attracted to the strong, silent type; I think I associated this with discipline and, in reaction to my father's undisciplined nature, had determined that the best match for me would be a lean army general with a strict budget and lifestyle. It took being burned by a few such men for me to realize a softer, gentler man would be better for me.

When we were just friends, I suggested that Marvin seek a male mentor, and even though he resisted at first ("West Indian men don't spill their guts to other men," he said), he soon saw the value of it and sought one out; that man helped Marvin tremendously during our courtship and was his best man at our wedding! He also has male buddies whom he likes to hang out with, and I appreciate that. I didn't then and don't now want to be his only friend or the only one with whom he is transparent, and he sees the value of that, too.

He also said he was sorry with such ease that, on many occasions, I shook my head in astonishment at his emotional maturity and security. I wondered that such men existed, and my respect for him grew exponentially.

5. Has a good work ethic, is not lazy, and is respected at his job by his boss and colleagues

I had a boyfriend who hated his job, got fired, and collected unemployment for months. I learned the same thing from him that I had learned from my father: Men who hate their jobs are miserable to be around. I realized that I didn't just want a provider; I wanted a career man, one who had found his niche, loved his job, worked hard, and made himself invaluable in his field. It wasn't really about his paycheck, although, realistically, I wanted it to be enough to support a family, but it was more about his joy level at work and his sense of accomplishment. I am sure some of this came from having a childhood marred by embarrassment about my father's odd minimum wage jobs.

Listening to Marvin talk about his research and his expertise in his particular field (he is a scientist), my heart swelled with pride, and one more piece of the puzzle slid into place.

6. Disciplined, but not legalistic, uptight, or bound up

7. Possessing high moral standards

Both six and seven speak to the same chamber of the heart. I wanted a man of principle, but not that strict army general I talked about. When I discovered that Marvin was (and is) an early riser who cooked nutritious meals (rather than frequenting fast food joints like a lot of bachelors I had known), had a savings account, and had slightly old-fashioned views about how men and women should behave together, my heart sang. He too didn't believe in married people having one-on-one friendships with people of the opposite sex. He cut off cable TV as a newly saved single man to guard his eyes and heart from the barrage of sexual images. He was always faithful to girlfriends and is actually more turned off than turned on by breast exposing tops and easy women. I discovered these things when we were just friends, and these traits and others caused me to fall in love with him deeply.

8. Committed to keeping our dating relationship pure; no hang-ups about sex; open and honest about it; not lustful; shows me (though he may notice other attractive women) that I am the "apple of his eye"; no wandering eyes

I dated a couple of guys who expected me to do all the work of keeping things on the straight and narrow, and I wanted a man who would do some of the work, too—indeed, who would actually take the lead in this area. I also had the putrid experience of being with guys who snuck glances at other women when they thought I wasn't looking. On the other hand, I had boyfriends who were so worried about lust that they practically viewed sex as sinful but necessary behavior to indulge in every once in a while with one's prudish, sexless wife. Yuck! I wanted a man who wanted me (yep, sexually), who had eyes only for me, and yet waited for me.

9. Spiritual leader; reads his Bible; knows how to get the Rhema

word of God; has a regular prayer life; wants to pray with me and read the Word together; takes the lead in spiritual matters with me; is prophetic and intuitive; calls me higher; encourages me to trust God; has something to give spiritually

I didn't just want a church-goer or a guy who spoke Christian-eeze; I wanted someone with a real relationship with the Lord. Someone who heard from God and had insights and revelation and got me thinking about deep stuff. There are so many shallow Christians out there, and I didn't want to marry one! I didn't want a ball and chain around my ankles, but rather wind in my spiritual sails—someone who would run this race of faith with me, neck-and-neck, rather than lagging behind, sluggish and unmotivated.

I got saved when I was eight; Marvin accepted Christ at thirty-five. I had lots of Scripture memorized and knew my way through the Bible. Marvin didn't know what was in the Old Testament and what was in the New. But he was a new, radical, zealous Christian who was not jaded by church politics. And he devoured the Word. We spent our dates talking about the Bible and what God had shown him. He learned quickly how to hear God's voice and discern His ways. My growth was long and slow; his fast and exciting.

10. Straight-forward personality; "black and white"; not overly analytical; sees it and does it; assertive; knows what he wants and goes after it

I had dated several indecisive men. They liked me but didn't know if they loved me or wanted to marry me. They liked their jobs but didn't know if they wanted to keep them. They liked their homes but constantly thought about moving. There was no stability. I had heard of men who, when they saw their future wives for the first time, knew they were going to marry them; that's what I wanted! No hemming and hawing, no weighing and waiting. I wanted my man to see the prize and run after it without compunction. And that's exactly what I got.

11. Dynamic and personable; easy to talk to; comfortable around people; not awkward; a people person; not a recluse

I'm a social person, and I wanted a man with whom I could go to parties and barbecues. I wanted a man who would fit in, be comfortable, and be just a regular guy, someone who would laugh with my friends and put them at ease. No geeks, recluses, or introverts. In truth, Marvin is a bit of a geek, he likes to be alone, and he's more private than I am, but he also has a social side and can handle himself very well around people.

12. Secure and mature; encourages me to "go for it"; not threatened by me being in the public eye or in leadership positions

Being a woman in ministry is challenging! The Church is still a man's world, and many men don't think women should even be in the pulpit. However, God made it clear to me that He's called me to be a teacher and to be in the public arena. My husband would have to not only deal with that but like it and encourage me in it.

Marvin loves it when I preach; he brags and boasts about me. He encourages me to take opportunities as they come, and he invests time and money in my gifts.

13. Physically bigger than I am: taller, strong, healthy and in good shape

I like wearing heels, I like dancing, and I like hugging. All three are easier with taller men. I also like guys who are somewhat athletic and who would go biking and walking with me. I'd be willing to do without such things, but since they were my only physical stipulations, I didn't feel too greedy asking for them!

Thankfully, Marvin is just the right height, and he's in great shape!

14. Values marriage and family; takes marriage seriously; wants to marry and is ready for its responsibilities and commitment; open to adoption

Many men have no desire to adopt children; they want to have their own or none at all but have closed hearts when it comes to adopting someone else's kid. Before we started dating, Marvin and I went to a fundraiser at a children's home. As we looked at a video on foster children, Marvin casually said, "I'd like to adopt someday." I took note!

15. Financially stable; has a good job and vision for his life, ministry, and future in general; not floundering; likes his job and

has a sense of purpose and calling

16. A romantic (Enjoys romantic things like good food, music, dancing, walking, talking, giving flowers, etc.)

17. A gentleman

The first time Marvin and I took a walk together, he insisted on walking on the outside, next to the traffic. He apologized for his old fashioned nature but wouldn't hear of it any other way. He also held doors, picked me up at home, and paid for dinner. And yet, he loved my mind, respected me as an equal, and never patronized me.

18. Has good manners but is down to earth; can mix with the upper and lower classes

My father taught me to hate pretense. Thus, I wanted my husband to be able to relate to blue collar, white collar, and no collar men. I have both rich and poor friends and can easily go from one side of the tracks to another. I wanted my husband to be able to do the same. Marvin lived up to this desire as well. Most people have no idea that he has a PhD because he's so down-to-earth, humble, and normal!

Your Turn

That's my list. You may value different things, but the important thing is that you have values! What are your standards? If you are younger, you may have to look more at a guy's potential than what he actually already has, but there should be some hard evidence, too! Maybe you're in college, and the guy you have your eye on doesn't have a savings account. No problem, but is he wise with money? Does he blow every extra cent on toys? If so, is he open to change, or will that be a constant source of tension? Maybe you're in your twenties, and your guy hasn't found the ideal job yet. That's OK, but does he have goals and desires? Is he working toward something, or is he apathetic, content with earning barely enough and remaining passionless? If your guy has dabbled in pornography, has he repented, asked a mentor for accountability, and removed any source of temptation from his life, or does he still toe the line and play with fire?

Remember, there's no such thing as a perfect man, but what is his heart like? Is it teachable, pliable, and soft? Or is it proud, obstinate, and closed?

As I mentioned before, this Scripture guided me and became a source of confirmation that Marvin was the One:

> *The Lord does not look at the things man looks at. Man looks at the outward appearance, but the Lord looks at the heart (1 Samuel 16:7).*

You should ultimately be physically attracted to the guy you marry, but the most important thing, the thing to examine and probe, is his heart.

ABOUT NICOLE C. DOYLEY

Nicole Doyley grew up in Brooklyn, New York, and then attended Dartmouth College, where she earned a BA in English. After graduation, she continued to live in New Hampshire, serving in full-time ministry for almost twenty years. In 2006, two weeks before her fortieth birthday, she married Marvin, her long-awaited Boaz. The couple now lives in Rochester, New York, with their two sons, Isaac and Benjamin. She is also the author of One: Racial Unity in the Body of Christ.

For more information or to contact the author, visit
www.ruthscompany.org